Dear Lovers—

Here is an unfinished book.
It is yet to be completed
by you. More important than
what I have written will be
what *you* write! Please take
the time—and love—to jot
beside the opening photos
your own private, special
moments. And as you read the
book, answer the questions
and talk about them with
each other. The purpose of
the book is to bring you
closer together. That's the
best thing you can do to
make your marriage great!

Happy writing (and reading)

Enjoy,

Chuck

Fr. Chuck Gallagher

Library of Congress Catalog
Card Number: 76-4329

Published by William H. Sadlier, Inc.,
New York, Chicago, Los Angeles and
Serendipity House, Box 461, Scottdale,
Pennsylvania 15683. Printed in U.S.A.

LOVE IS A COUPLE

by Fr. Chuck Gallagher, S.J.

edited and arranged by Bob and Lois Blewett

Marriage Encounter Resource Community

William H. Sadlier, Inc.
NEW YORK • CHICAGO • LOS ANGELES

Our love
is so special ...

It began the summer we met ...

... when everyday was just for us.

We committed ourselves to each other.

Apartment-fixing
was par for the course.

*A special Encounter
made our love
better than ever!*

Our love is exciting ...

to long, unexpected delays.

We can't stand
to be apart — ever.

We are happily-ever-aftering — forever!

The special moments of our love:

The day we met

What I liked most about you

The moment I knew you were the one!

My favorite date with you

Our craziest date

What I liked most about our wedding day

Our best honeymoon — so far

My favorite gift from you

The special signs you give me of your love

The thoughts we most like to share

Your most endearing quality

What brings us closest

My wildest dreams for us!

My listening to you is for _you_
and benefits us both.

1

LISTENING

What is the difference between hearing and listening?

Your answer:

Every couple of weeks or so, Margaret would ask Bill to take her out for dinner. Most of the time he'd do it. He thought she wanted to get away from the kids, eat a meal when she didn't have to wash the dishes, be away from the house after being tied down day after day.

One evening he came home particularly tense and tired. It had been a difficult day at the office, but he was tense because he had agreed that morning to take Margaret out to dinner that evening. So he said, "Look Margaret, I'm just beat tonight and I'm not up to going out. I'll feed the kids. You call up a girlfriend and go out with her."

Margaret said, "OK," and she started to go over to the phone. Then Bill realized that even though she had said OK, it wasn't OK. There had been disappointment in her voice. It really got to him. His heart melted.

He went over and took the phone out of her hand. "Margaret, what's the matter?"

"Nothing."

"Oh, but there is. Let's talk about it. I really want to know."

"Bill, I don't want to go out with a girlfriend. I was looking forward all day to going out with you for dinner."

"Yes," said Bill," I know that you've had the kids on your back and Timmy and Bill have been sick all week and it does get to be a drag stuck in the house. I know you need to get out. Why can't you go out with Mary or Fran and have a nice time?"

"But Bill, that isn't the point. Yes, I'd like to get out, and it's nice to dress up and go to a nice restaurant and have somebody wait on me for a change, and not be rushed. But the nicest thing about going out to dinner is that it's with you. I get so little time to spend with you. I want to be with you and talk a little bit and look at you and just enjoy your company."

Bill shook his head, "What a dummy I am. All these years that I've been taking you out to dinner I thought it was the dinner you wanted—and it was me! That's really nice. C'mon, Margaret, let's go. And you're going to get plenty of me!"

When Bill's hearing changed to listening, he found out how Margaret felt and their relationship grew.

Hearing is the sensory-perception experience by which sound is transmitted to me. When I hear words, I receive the message that is being communicated. I also know the logical consequences and some of the implications of what is being said.

There are times, however, when sounds reach me but I don't really receive the message.

A classroom or business situation requires that information and facts be heard. An interpersonal relationship requires hearing as only the first step to listening. Listening involves far more. It demands that I be aware of *you*—not just of what you're saying but of who you are and, most especially, of who we are to each other. In listening, it's not good enough for me to be able to repeat your words. I have to know what they mean to you, how they are affecting you, and how important it is for you to communicate to me.

Hearing concerns itself with information. Listening, on the other hand, has to do with persons. It concerns itself with you, not merely with what you're saying. When I listen to you, I'm *caring about you.* I want to be present to you. In hearing, information is dominant; in listening, conformation is dominant. In listening, I have to allow you to affect me, to get to me, to touch me and have an influence upon me. In hearing, I merely take in information and evaluate it objectively. When I'm listening, I'm never objective. I'm always on your side. I'm always *for* you. I'm always reaching out to you, trying to experience the you who is present in the words you are communicating to me.

So, for listening to take place, there has to be personal involvement. I can't be standing outside evaluating what is going on between us. I have to be conscious of you, responsive to you, and eager for you to be in touch with me. I don't expect the message itself to turn me on or even to make much sense to me. You already make sense to me. You are important to me, and I am turned on to you.

I cannot listen to you without the whole of me being involved. I can hear you with only half an ear. While I'm hearing, I can filter out what is unimportant, irrelevant or distracting. While I'm listening to you, I can't be selective. Nothing is irrelevant, nothing unimportant, nothing distracting, about you.

Hearing is for *my* sake, for *my* purposes, for what *I'm* going to get out of it. Maybe I just find the subject interesting, or I judge that you deserve to be heard. All these things can motivate me to give you attention. Listening, on the other hand, is for *your* sake. It's for what *you* get out of it, for what happens to *you* as a result of my listening. Hearing is determined by what goes on inside me, what effect it has on me. Listening is determined by what goes on inside you, what my listening does for you.

Lane and Terry were sitting on the couch one evening just enjoying a time of quiet when, for no reason at all, he turned and looked at her. Suddenly he said, "Y'know, Terry dear, you're really beautiful." She caught herself from passing it off, because it struck her that he meant it. The realization took her breath away. Neither of them said a word. Then Lane's eyes filled up and the tears rolled down his cheeks. He said he had told her many times before, but he'd not been able to get through to her. There was relief in him now that Terry had finally listened, and he was thrilled. It was a precious moment for both of them.

Would you consider yourself a good listener?   *Your answer:*

I may feel that I am not a good listener because I do most of the talking or other people have told me that I'm not listening. Maybe I find I am frequently distracted when I think I'm listening to other people speak. Maybe I can't repeat what others have said. These are indications that my listening capabilities have not been developed to a very high degree.

However, most of us judge ourselves to be rather good listeners. We may not listen well all the time, but at least we do so when it's important. Besides, we don't say very much. Many people think that the silent person is the one who is listening. Actually, without saying a word, Silent Sam and Taciturn Tessie may be just as uninvolved as any noisy and loud-mouthed person. They may not be saying anything, but in their minds they're talking back to the other person or putting in their own judgments. Or they may even take in what is said—just hear the words—and get a certain amount of enjoyment out of it. Many people get the reputation of being good listeners when, at best, they're only good hearers!

Of course, the silent person could possibly be sleeping inside. His eyes may be wide open and he may be smiling, but inside he's in another world, floating in space. There is no listening going on there at all; he is totally absorbed in his own thoughts. He's probably carrying on a conversation with himself. There is no involvement with the other person.

Do you consider yourself to be a good listener when the

situation calls for it? However, maybe even then you are more involved with the subject than the person. We listen to a *person*. We never listen to a *subject,* although we may hear. Maybe we meet an expert in a certain field and we need as much information and advice in that area as possible. Or maybe we're desperate and don't know which way to turn, so we'll be attentive to anybody. But in these situations we're looking for solutions to our problems; we're not listening to the other person.

The real measure of whether or not I'm a good listener is how much understanding—or empathy—you experience when you're with me. It's true, of course, that sometimes you only want to get things off your chest, so you feel better after you've been talking to me, no matter how I've listened.

When somebody is very upset, I may pay attention to him in order to make him feel better. If he is upset with me, I may pay attention because I want him to stop reprimanding me. Paying attention in the first case is good and beautiful in itself. Paying attention in the second case is a response to a situation. In either case listening is not taking place in the full sense of the term, because I'm not responding to the person.

From a good hearer the speaker goes away satisfied. From a good listener the speaker never, in one sense, goes away—he is always "present" to his listener.

**Do you ever listen
with your eyes?**

Your answer:

We usually consider listening to be restricted to the function of the ears. If I get the words right and understand what the other person is saying and don't allow my prejudices to distort what I'm hearing, then I feel I'm a good listener. But listening is something with which my whole personhood is involved. I try to discover the other person, and I can't do that with just one faculty, one sense. I have to listen to you with the whole of me.

A husband or wife communicates a lot by body language to a sensitive spouse. One can tell whether the other is tense or nervous or upset, by the way he's standing or moving, or by the look on his face. Sometimes the tone of what is said is casual or even light-hearted, but the body symptoms reveal a different inner state. Maybe the wife is moving around nervously; maybe her shoulders are slumped, which shows the husband she is discouraged. Possibly she exhibits mannerisms that only he knows, indicating that a fire is burning inside her.

Frequently, especially in a husband-wife relationship, the words that are spoken are not important at all. One has to be looking at the other to see behind the words. Maybe the body language is revealing a plea for attention, an aching loneliness, or a searching for companionship. Maybe a sparkle in the eyes is announcing a bubbling joy wanting to be shared.

Pete and Fran always seem to wind up disagreeing over money. One day they were talking about going on a vacation. Fran wanted one that happened to involve quite a bit of money. But they did have the money. Fran couldn't understand why Pete was always so adamant about not spending money. Then she caught a glimpse of the fear in his eyes. She stopped arguing and listened. She discovered that Pete was desperately afraid of leaving her unprovided for and he had an urgency to save enough money for a rainy day. She realized then that she had been hearing his arguments but not listening to him. Seeing his fear changed the way she approached money from then on in. It wasn't that she stopped spending money or having a desire for a nice vacation, but she was able to get beyond the issue to what was going on inside Pete.

What it comes down to is that I'm not going to feel listened to, no matter how well the faculty of hearing is being used, if you are not taking notice of me, not looking at me. There is no way I can be convinced that you are listening to me if your eyes are everyplace else—or looking at me only intermittently.

One good sharp look to see how I am is not enough either. You've tucked what I looked like in the back of your mind. However, the message that I'm communicating by body language is constantly being modified and changed; therefore, your eyes

Everything about you
is important to me.

have to be constantly on me if you are really listening.

We don't always look at the person talking to us, because we recognize instinctively that if we do we're going to get more involved. So we keep our eyes busy elsewhere. If we use our eyes to listen we know we're going to get drawn into the other person. We're going to know too much. We don't consciously make the decision to keep eyes off; we've been trained to it. And we often don't want to care that much or that intensely. We have our own worries, our own troubles.

In the marriage ceremony we say, "With all my worldly goods I thee endow." The better vow would be, "With all my senses I thee endow." We don't give all our senses to each other. Most of the time we give only halfhearted attention to hearing each other and probably less than halfhearted attention to *listening* to each other.

Do you ever listen
with your hands?

Your answer:

In order to discover our spouse, we can't listen with only our ears and not even with only our ears and eyes. We have to listen with our hands as well.

As a priest I go to many wakes and always try to offer what consolation I can to the widow. Before I leave the funeral parlor I make a practice of going to the widow and asking her how she is and how things are with her. I honestly try to listen to what she says. I look at her for telltale signs—a trembling lower lip or a welling up of tears in the eyes. But I've learned that listening calls for more. I put my arm around her and listen to her back muscles. Frequently the words are along the line of "I'm fine," "I'm doing quite well" or "I'm all right." But the stiffness of the muscles or the wetness of the back of the blouse lets you really know what's going on inside.

We can determine far more about what's inside the other person when we're touching than when we're not. (Often in counseling I deliberately choose to keep myself separate from the other person when I want to be objective, to analyze what is going on between us, or to discover what is inside the other person or inside me, short of being involved. I may need to get a position across or a decision made.)

Touching creates an intimacy. It may appear very casual on the surface, but when I touch you and allow you to touch me there is a commitment involved. There are not many people we touch—certainly not for any extended period. Most forms of touch are ritualistic. We shake people's hands or give them a hug or a kiss. Unfortunately, touching can be ritualistic inside marriage, too, often taking place only on certain occasions or for particular purposes. Actually, one of the most important reasons for touching in marriage is to listen better to each other!

One of the ways we distract ourselves is by keeping our hands busy with things—straightening up the room, shuffling the pages of the newspaper, or fixing a clock. Even though I perform a purely mechanical operation, a certain amount of my attention is taken by it. When I put my hands on you—when I hold your hand or put my arm around your shoulders or touch your cheek—I'm saying that I'm here, here in the most tangible way possible. You can feel my presence. Furthermore, if I'm touching you, it helps me to keep my eyes on you. I keep noticing you.

Another advantage of touching is that it helps you to reveal more of yourself. There is nothing better than a gentle touch to give you confidence, a sense of being wanted. In that kind of environment, you can be more open. You can reveal more of yourself. It takes away some of the fear of possible rejection.

Moreover, when I touch you, you communicate a lot about yourself to me, in a way that allows me to experience you more deeply and more meaningfully than I possibly could by just hearing your words or seeing you. The trembling under my fingers, the tense back muscles, the rigid jaw, the cold hands, or the goose bumps on the forearm tell me what's going on inside you.

Actually, my hands touching you allow you to "get to me." Isn't that what listening is all about? There are so many things that can be said when we're touching each other. There are also many things that no longer have to be said! We can experience deep personal understanding when we touch.

Do you let the other person reveal himself?

Your answer:

Human beings are very peculiar. We're constantly searching for a deep personal relationship with our husband or wife. Yet many things we do show that we're really afraid of that kind of relationship and try to avoid it. We say with our mouths that there is nothing we want more than to be really close, really aware of each other. But our actions belie that claim. We set up many barriers to communion.

One of the biggest barriers to communication is our interrupting each other. We might interrupt because we honestly think we know what the other person is going to say and we're not patient enough to let him say it his way. We want to shortcut it for him. We want to show him that we "understand" him. So we pop in when he's halfway through. We tell him we know what he means.

We may also interrupt because we're not really interested in what our spouse is saying. We don't want to talk about it all night, so we try to get the conversation on some other topic. Maybe we have something that is much more interesting to us, so we introduce our topic. We may do this either subtly or with a crash.

Another reason behind an interruption may be that something is weighing heavily on my mind. I want to talk about it, and I want the other person to listen. I don't want to do the listening this time. Therefore I switch the talk to my problem. I can excuse myself by saying, "I'm always doing the listening. Tonight I want to talk." Or I may feel that the other person is by nature the listener and we always make better progress when I do the talking.

Another way to interrupt is to be very nice. Janet really wants to be listened to, wants to feel understood, but as soon as Carl hears what she is saying, he gives a solution. He promises he'll change or do something to please her, or he'll stop doing whatever it is that upsets her. However, that is not what Janet is talking about; she just wants to reach Carl, get inside him. But he doesn't want to be gotten inside of, he doesn't want to listen to who she is. He just hears her complaint or her desire and says, "I'll do whatever you want." On the surface he seems very accommodating, but he's really turning her off.

Often we interrupt non-verbally rather than by introducing another topic of conversation. We let our eyes wander, or busy ourselves doing something around the house, or pick up a newspaper. Or we stand there patiently "listening" but obviously

Don't just hear my words — notice me!

waiting for the other person to run down so we can go about what we're more interested in.

This non-verbal turn-off can be done very nicely. We can make ourselves busy doing something for the other person, yet we are distracting ourselves from him.

I can also interrupt you by showing you a lot of affection. I give you a big hug and a kiss or pat you on the back. I want you to feel that I adore you, but it comes across to you as pity and an attempt to make it all better, and you feel that I don't care about you at that moment.

Sometimes we interrupt by our body language—it might be a mannerism like tapping a pencil or twisting a ring. It might be the sag of our body that indicates we're not caught up in what is being said. We're just waiting for it to be over with. Even while we're not saying a word, we can be communicating volumes to our spouse. It's up to us to get ourselves out of the way and listen, truly listen to the person who means more to us than anyone else in the world.

Do you listen with your answer running?

Your answer:

Sometimes we can be so bursting with what is inside us that even though we haven't begun to speak, we're obviously just waiting for the other person to be finished. We sometimes pop in the first moment he takes a breath!

A husband and wife have talked over many things at great length and sometimes in much depth. So the first sentence out of our spouse's mouth convinces us that we know what the whole thought is going to be. Or maybe it reminds us of something we wanted to say the last time we were talking about the same subject, so we don't listen at all to what is being said. We just wait for an opportunity to get in our two-cents' worth.

We don't mean to be harsh or malicious. We don't have any bad motives. It's simply that we're so full of what is going on inside of us that we get distracted from what is being said. It happens time and time again. We need to use some discipline and put ourselves aside in order to focus in on the other person and what he's saying.

Often as soon as someone says something that triggers an answer in me, I want to solve his problem, answer his questions, or give him advice or a piece of information. Many times I come out with the piece of information and my spouse injects, "That's what I just said." I end up with egg on my face and a big "Oh" on my lips.

Part of our difficulty is that we think we have to have answers to everything. Actually, a personal relationship is not predicated on solutions to problems or answers to questions. Our highest goal should be to understand each other, get close to each other, experience each other. To reach that goal we need to be open to each other, revealing ourselves—and listening. To communicate, we don't have to have an answer for our spouse. We just have to be aware of him, tasting and touching him. In our society, we're highly trained to be analytical. We're forever wanting to find some better way to do things. We want to present some cure, some improvement, some advice, to make the other person better off. But in the communication between the husband and wife, the most important thing is not just to be better off, it's to be understood!

Do you get distracted while you're listening?   *Your answer:*

If I go out of the house one morning and trip over the front step, it's an accident. If I trip over the step the next day, it may still be an accident. But if it occurs the third day—then I have to ask myself why. I have to start looking; there might be a loose plank or a nail sticking up, or something wrong with my shoe.

If I find myself being distracted from you time and time again, it's not an accident. It isn't as simple as, "I'm not paying attention because I was distracted." I'm choosing not to pay attention. I don't *want* to pay attention.

We often don't see that our communicating with each other demands a great deal of practice and discipline. A good marital relationship doesn't just happen. One key to having a good relationship is to decide to listen to our spouse. There is no way that listening is going to take place unless we deliberately choose to listen. Too often we leave our listening up to circumstances. We'll begin to listen if both of us feel drawn together, when a sort of magic makes us close. That is like saying, "If I happen to notice the step, then I won't trip over it." So it's a good thing to take notice of the step, because otherwise I fall flat on my face. Wouldn't it be foolish of me to make no attempt to notice the step?

Too often we're falling flat on our faces in our communication because we're not taking notice of each other. We excuse ourselves on the theory that we are distracted, that we don't mean not to take notice. But we do mean not to take notice because we haven't really tried to be attentive! We have to make that decision.

After a number of years of marriage, a husband and wife know what distracts them from listening. She is always busy cleaning the house or washing the dishes or fixing something for the kids. He's always watching TV or reading the newspaper or helping the kids with their homework. Or maybe it's paying the bills, or listening for the slightest noise from the children's bedroom, or just sleeping. Whatever it is, their experience reveals to them what distracts them from paying attention to each other. We can say to ourselves that we're just not good at listening. Nobody is. Everybody has to choose to listen and discipline himself to do it. There is no easy way; it doesn't just happen. Distractions are a dime a dozen. If it isn't one thing, it'll be another. However, distractions are not the problem. They are just a means whereby we avoid facing each other.

We cultivate distractions because we have not deliberately chosen to make our relationship a deep one. Maybe we're afraid of getting too close, afraid of bringing up hurts from the past, or afraid that we are so bound up in our business or children that our relationship can't be as attractive as we once hoped it would be. But the bottom line is that we haven't made the decision to cultivate a deep, meaningful relationship. Until we get more involved with each other and learn to be attentive to each other, we'll find a gnawing dissatisfaction and a loneliness continuously present. Listening will be an intermittent thing that happens only when the spirit moves us. A couple can be stronger than the distractions, and their relationship will have new dimensions.

Do you assume that you know what the other person is going to say?

Your answer:

After a time of being married, husbands and wives know each other's stories. They know what the other person is going to say before he opens his mouth. When anything happens, one spouse automatically knows what the other's reaction will be. When they talk together they fall into the trap of believing they really don't have to listen. They've been this route before. They know exactly what the other person's position is.

When their wives start to talk, how many husbands get a look on their faces that says to all the world, "I've heard that song before"? When their husbands begin to talk, how many wives by their expressions say, loud and clear, "Not again! We've been through all this before."

We may not get angry; we may be patient and just tolerate the whole thing. We don't let ourselves get excited about it. We expect it. We busy our minds with something else. It is a typical husband-and-wife situation.

Here's a startling thought. Maybe one of the reasons someone is saying the same thing again and again is because he wasn't

We've been married long enough to talk about everything, really!

listened to in the first place. Oh, sure, maybe the other person heard what the position was. He may have it memorized. It could be true that the position hasn't changed over the years. But we can't listen to a *position!* We listen to a *person!* The person is always fresh, always new.

Even though we could often complete the other's sentence, we might be surprised at its conclusion if we let him complete his own thought. The conclusion may be different from what we had expected. However, because we have finished the other's sentences for so many years, he may well have given up trying to say what he wanted to say. He says to himself, "I really want to say 'white.' But she thinks I'm going to say 'black.' OK. Let it be that way." Or she is saying to herself, "I know that whenever we talk about money he's certain that I'm going to be asking for more. Actually, I just want to talk about how I understand the pressure that is on him, and to share a little bit of my own pressure. I don't need any more money, but since he's convinced I do, there's no point in trying to go into it. He's not going to listen, because he feels so sure of what I'm going to say!"

Many husbands and wives end up with nothing to say to each other because they're convinced they've already said it all. When they talk they play the other person's speaking part as well as their own.

We may say that we don't do that. Well, we may not do it as overtly and as crudely as somebody else, but we do it! Let's take another look at the person we're living with and let him say what he really wants to say—all of it. Many things have affected him in the years that we've been married. Maybe he's changed a great deal in the last few months. There is so much that can make our relationship exciting if we listen!

Are you closed to certain topics?   *Your answer:*

Every one of us has areas of conversation that we don't like to go into. Maybe we've been on a topic before and didn't get anywhere. Maybe a certain subject has been a source of problems between us, or one of us gets too upset when we talk about it. It might be a mother, a brother, money, sex, religion—or almost anything. Every couple has a mental niche in which they store many topics that are brought out only when necessary, taken care of as quickly as possible, and put back in the niche again.

We may not even realize we're doing it. We should ask ourselves what topics we don't discuss much. Of course we don't discuss Red China or international finance or multi-national corporations all the time. But what normal, personal human topics—husband-and-wife topics—do we seldom discuss or never discuss in depth? Their absence indicates there is something there for us to talk about! Is there some kind of barrier preventing us from being open with each other and going deeply into those topics?

Sometimes we may think we're very open on certain subjects. Sex, for instance. But we don't go into it deeply. We talk about it in terms of what other people do, or in reference to a magazine article, or how to educate our children about sex. We haven't discussed it in terms of our relationship, how we feel about it, what sex means to us, what we want out of it, and what we're missing. It may well be that one or the other has thought about trying to do so but is afraid that the spouse is going to see it as a personal attack. The husband may have settled for the present situation because in his mind good girls just don't like sex all that much. After all, that is why he married her, because she was a good girl. He doesn't feel free to talk to her about that area of their lives. Or maybe he looks on himself as a failure, so he avoids any talk about sex because then his failure will come out in the open, and he doesn't want that.

Ralph and Sally had a very good relationship with one another and they talked over most things. It just seemed that they never got around to talking much about sex. Sally, though, after a while began to recognize that any time the subject did come up she was uneasy about it and turned to something else as quickly as possible. Then she realized that after all, sex was something very important between the two of them and not to talk about it didn't make much sense. It wasn't that they had a problem or anything. It was simply that the more that she could understand Ralph and he could understand her, the better it had to be for the two of them. One evening she sat down with him and said, "Don't you think, Ralph, that we've been married long enough to talk about sex?" She told him that she had become aware that she had been avoiding the topic and that she really wanted to understand him better and wanted to talk more openly about it. Because she loved him so much, she didn't want there to be any distance between them in this area.

They found themselves laughing at each other because they were like two little school kids. Because of Sally's courageous act of love, Ralph was able to talk to her about his uncertainties—how he sometimes wondered whether he was attractive to her and whether sex was important to her. He was able to share with her his being lonely in sex sometimes because of his insecurity and the uncertainties. This really surprised Sally because she thought he had it all together and sex was no problem for him, it was just a problem for her. They didn't try to solve any problems or change anything. Just the experience of being more aware of each other made a difference. They had a great feeling of warmth toward each other and a whole new world opened up for them.

Probably all couples talk about money, but most often they talk about it in terms of how little they have, their bills, their financial pressures, how high taxes are, or the terrible rate of inflation. They may talk about their savings account or their investment plan. But they don't talk in terms of how money is affecting *them*: what their attitude is toward money, or what effect money is having on their relationship. They don't talk about their fears, their insecurities; about how much of his manhood is tied up in being a good provider, how it affects her when she says no to the children's wants, what she thinks of herself when she sees other women dressing better than she does.

In most cases, a topic is avoided not because it is too tough or because it poses a problem with no solution, but because the husband or wife feels the other is not going to listen. In some cases one believes that if he does listen he's going to have to do something he doesn't want to do. But wait a minute. Listening has nothing to do with making decisions; it has to do with *experiencing* the other person.

Another reason we eliminate certain topics from our conversation is that they mean a great deal to one or both of us and we dont' see eye to eye on them. They're a bit risky to get into. Those topics take in whole areas of our lives where there is no understanding between us. Hurts are involved.

There is a way to overcome the situation. We can talk about the subject in great depth, listening to each other not in terms of changing the other's mind but of experiencing what is meaningful to him. Not because the topic is a major one or my spouse's position on it is correct, but because I love him.

You help me understand myself!

If we are not wide open in our communication, if we are not willing to talk about everything with each other, we are limiting our areas of relationship. We're saying, "I love you and I'll be very open with you and you can know the whole me—except when it comes to your mother, your political views—or whatever."

There was one subject that Ben didn't like to have come up between him and Melissa, and that was her friend Fay. Melissa seemed to do anything Fay told her to do, especially when it came to the children. And every time Melissa was out with Fay she came home irritable and not herself. It was always a bad scene. So he decided not to say anything and to put up with it.

But one day he realized that wasn't working out either. Fay was between them like a cloud. He also realized that if he were going to bring up the subject he would have to be very gentle and not attack Melissa. He would not try to change her, but just share his feelings. It was hard for him to do it. He was still angry at Fay. He realized he had to take his eyes off Fay and put them on Melissa. He told her they had something to talk about and he wasn't so cocksure about the solution as he used to be. He promised not to be closed and blind to what she would say and to try to listen. He went on, "We honestly have to talk about this because it's hurting us and neither of us wants that. I promise to be gentle and understanding so that we can talk about Fay calmly, keeping *us* and our *love* foremost in our minds."

That was a good first step. Ben and Melissa have not resolved every aspect of the problem to their complete satisfaction, but now that they're talking about it, the whole tone is better.

The closing off of topics between husband and wife either leads to our keeping our own counsel (and the subject churns within us) or we start talking to other people about it. We actually experience more understanding from someone else than we do from our spouse. There is a breach in our relationship. We may accept it, saying we understand because "nobody can be open to everything." But that is an intellectual understanding; we don't really understand with our hearts. For the situation, more often than not, leads to the statement, "My wife doesn't understand me," or, "My husband doesn't listen to me."

We need to talk about the off-limits topic, not to settle it, but in order to experience what is going on inside of us about it. Then we can be in communion. In other words, if the wife's mother is the delicate subject, it isn't the mother that the husband wants to experience, but his wife! He needs to know what is going on inside her because of her mother. If the girl has a tenderness in her heart for her mother, she needs to share that with him, not in order to persuade him that his bad experience with her mother was his fault or that he has to change, but to help him feel some of the tenderness that is in her heart. On the other hand, if she's having a running battle with her mother, she doesn't need to get him stirred up against the mother; she needs to have him understand the hurt and pain she's experiencing because of the separation from her mother. That is what he has to take on.

If money is the topic, the couple needs to get the budget straightened out, or to reach agreement about how much money should be put in the bank and how much should be spent immediately. She needs to grasp the fear that grips his guts about leaving her and the kids unprovided for; not so that she will spend less money or be upset when one of the children spills milk and wastes money, but so that she can understand him. Her listening seriously can help him open up, and their "coupleness" will be reinforced joyously.

What is your biggest defect in listening?

Your answer:

Maybe I know that my biggest problem in listening is that I only "hear" and don't even try to listen. Or I allow any number of things to distract me; or I half listen—I hear with my ears but let my eyes and hands wander. Or I listen with my answer running, or fill in the other person's sentences. Maybe there are some things I won't talk about or listen to. Maybe my biggest defect is not being interested in listening, not being willing to put any effort into it.

On the other hand, I may be a talker, always wanting to be listened to. Or maybe my problem lies in thinking that I'm already a great listener. I think I'm sensitive and pay attention all the time. I think the other person has to learn to listen to me. That's probably the biggest defect of all, because then there's no hope. I'm stuck and don't even know it.

Another defect is the unwillingness to give listening the priority it deserves. I may excuse myself on the basis that I'm doing my best—"no one is perfect"—I'm just not a good listener and that's the way it is. But listening is definitely an important aspect of communication, and communication is vital to marriage.

It's also possible that I just follow my feelings when it comes to listening. If I'm in a listening mood, then I'll pay attention to you. If I'm not, then I'm not going to do anything to overcome my mood. If I feel close, or warm, or attracted to you, then anything you say will be important to me. If I don't have those feelings, if I feel the least bit distant from you, that has to be straightened out before I will listen to you. Maybe the distance could be removed by my listening!

Do we demand a 50-50 trade? Too many times we say, "I'll listen if you listen." That is not the point. The only listening I'm responsible for is my own. I can't demand that my husband or wife listen as a fair exchange. My commitment is to listen to my spouse regardless of whether or not he is listening to me. It's harder that way, but that is the reality.

Maybe we insist that other minimum requirements be fulfilled before we listen. "If you don't speak to me in an acceptable tone of voice, I'm not going to listen to you." But maybe the tone of voice is indicative of the other person's appeal to me to listen. Maybe it is the only way he can get through to me. "Unless you're nice to me I won't listen to you." "Unless you say the things I want to hear or say them the way I want to hear them, I won't listen to you." "I'll listen to you only when I have nothing else to do or when nothing else is attracting my attention." "I'll listen to you but only up to a certain hour; after that I want to relax and go to bed." In other words, we tend to set up all sorts of conditions before we'll agree to listen or even make the attempt to listen. What a difference open, generous listening would bring to our relationship!

Is your listening active or passive?

Your answer:

As long as I keep my ears clear of wax and pay attention to the words being said, I think I'm listening. But listening is not a passive experience, it is an active one. It is active in drawing you out. Many times you can't get your feelings and thoughts out by yourself. You need me. You need my encouragement and the verbalized and non-verbalized evidence that I am paying attention. You need to know I am listening. You also need to be helped and prodded and encouraged by my understanding as we go along. I need to question, "Is this what you mean?" "How are you feeling while you're saying this?" "Exactly what is going on inside you?" "Am I getting this clear?" All these questions have to be brought out in order for true listening to occur on the person level.

Once after giving a talk I remember meeting a teenage girl who angrily objected not so much to what I said as to what I didn't say. I began to defend myself. I explained that I didn't particularly disagree with the position she was holding, but I was addressing a different topic. I went on like this for some time, when suddenly she burst into tears. It was only then I saw her as a person. Instead of attacking her position, I finally began to get a sense of the values that she was expressing. I tried to help her explain them. I needed to look at what was behind her words and support her. As I did, her whole attitude changed and she left smiling and happy.

To be a good listener it's not enough to not interrupt; it's not enough to put in the appropriate acknowledgments at the right times and to say something sympathetic or give advice when the other person has finished.

In other words, listening is not just assimilating another person's revelation, it is actively participating in the revelation. A person has difficulty revealing himself by himself. It's not just a matter of letting everything hang out. You need my cooperation in order to reveal yourself.

The revelation itself is a very tenuous thing. It's a great risk for you to tell me what is going on inside you. If you're the silent type, you may not know how to talk about yourself. All along, during the process of the revelation, I have to be an active participant. I have to be helpful to you and show that I'm really interested, that I care, and that I am awed by your goodness in sharing yourself with me.

It's for my own sake, too, that I have to be that involved. I can't digest in one lump the fullness of you. It's only if I taste you as you gradually reveal yourself, only if I'm fully a part of your revelation, that I will be able to have true comprehension, awareness and understanding of you.

One of our difficulties is that we cheap-shot listening. We make it something so much less than it is. Actually, listening is one of the highest faculties of man, a wonderful gift, one of the most magnificent powers that God has given us. It has an incredible effect. A husband or wife who experiences being listened to is in seventh heaven!

What is your greatest talent in listening?   *Your answer:*

What do I do to help my beloved know that he is understood? What qualities of mine touch him?

The temptation is to shrug and say that I'm not much of a listener. But if I let it go at that, it's a cop-out. I'm telling other people to not expect me to listen. Then I'm never going to be any better than "not bad." One way to improve is to find out what I'm doing wrong and to correct it. Another way is to find out what I'm doing right and to improve on that! We have to have a certain awareness of our own worth in order to exercise our talents well.

Maybe you honestly try to listen. The point is not whether you always succeed, but that you are making a sincere effort. Possibly you are very sensitive to your partner, and have a deep understanding of him. You know how important listening is to him, and because you love him you want to offer this gift. Maybe you have patience, so you avoid interrupting even though your partner goes round and round before getting to the point.

Your particular talent could be the active interest you take in the other person and what is going on inside him, or a gentleness that encourages him to risk revealing himself. It could be that you have the gift of empathy that enables you to feel with the other person.

Whatever your special abilities are, be aware of them. Celebrate them! See how you can develop them further and put them at the service of your spouse more and more.

If you find it difficult to determine what your good qualities in listening are, ask your spouse. He probably understands you better than you understand yourself and is more generous in his appraisal of you than you are. (Even if you think you know what your special ability is, ask your partner anyway! He will almost certainly help you appreciate that quality more, and you'll see how important it is to him.)

Do you ask your spouse to help you listen better?   *Your answer:*

Listening is not a private personal ability a man or woman brings to marriage. There is, of course, an individual dimension to listening, but it is not exclusively the province of either one. Both have to help develop the other's listening. It is true to a degree that listening is something *I* have to do better. *I* have to change. I have to see what I'm doing right and what I'm doing wrong; I

It's when we
go out for coffee
that we can talk
about the most
serious things.

have to make the decision to do better at it, and I have to work on it myself. But you can help me know whether or not I'm succeeding in my self-improvement plan and tell me what matters to you.

Listening takes two to accomplish, not simply in the sense that there has to be a talker and a listener, but that both parties have to be personally involved. If I honestly and sincerely want to be a better listener, I have to bring you into the process. I can talk it over with you to see my strong points and how to develop them further, also to see my weak points and how to overcome them. I need to ask, what do I do that makes you feel understood, close, warm, protected? What am I doing that interferes with your experience of being understood?

We have to recognize that there is no such thing as *general* listening. Every act of listening is *custom-made.* In any husband-wife relationship, the listening is specific and personalized. Your wife or husband has to be listened to in a unique way, one that is meaningful to him. Consequently, your spouse has to help you formulate the special way of listening you're trying to develop for him. He shouldn't only encourage you, nor simply inform you whether your listening is working or not, but define what listening actually is in his terms. You are to listen to this particular person with whom you are in relationship in the way that is meaningful to him, with the qualities that make him aware that you have a sympathetic ear and an empathetic heart. Only he can tell you how to listen to him. So if you're really serious about listening, you have to go to the other person. You have to let him form your listening pattern, then you will know the specific practices and techniques that create the environment in which he can be most open to you.

Mike and Cathy were talking one day about how they best listen to each other. Cathy told Mike that he listens best for her when he just lets her finish what she wants to say, without asking her a question. She teased Mike about her having only a 50% chance of being listened to by him. Half the time he had the television on or a book or a pen in his hand.

Cathy explained how it makes such a difference to her if they don't just concentrate on the *subject* but get down to what their *feelings* are as individual persons. She liked him to hold her hand or put his arm around her, but she didn't really want to be enveloped by him because then she didn't believe she was being listened to, she felt then he was only giving his sympathy. Another thing Cathy noticed was that a lot of times Mike was in high gear and obviously thinking about something else or making plans. But when he's calm and sitting down quietly with her, then she feels listened to.

Mike told Cathy it's when she does more talking that he feels listened to, that when she doesn't say anything he's at his wit's end. He just doesn't know where he is with her. Mike told her how her gentle touches gave him confidence to continue talking openly with her.

Having no interruptions is very important to Mike. He wants her to put the little things aside, the distractions that take her attention away from him. When those distractions intrude, then he feels that he has to start all over again from the beginning because he's lost his train of thought and he's sure she doesn't know what he's just said. They had a good laugh together and learned more about each other than they had for a long time.

The best way of listening is more than following all sorts of general principles that seem to make sense. It's being fine-tuned to the other person. Your spouse has to tell you what really makes your listening come through with no interference. Then you can listen his way, not yours. After all, when you listen, it is not for your sake; it's not for what you get out of it. It's for your partner's sake, for what he gets out of it.

What can you do to help your spouse listen better?

Your answer:

I can't just demand that you listen to me. Putting the whole burden on you, leaving it all up to you, will not work. I have to take an active role in helping you listen to me. You really can't

45

listen to me without my participation, my cooperation. It's obvious that I need to say things clearly and be honest and revelatory in my speech. But I also need to help in the formation of your listening habits.

I have to communicate to you what helps me to be at ease and open. Maybe your gentle pattern of speech helps me get everything out that I want to express. Maybe your touch reassures me that you care enough to be involved in what I'm trying to say.

I also have to tell you what you might be doing that turns me off, that makes me think I'm not being listened to. Or maybe something makes me feel I'm being judged or that you are not interested. It could be a tone of voice or a look on the face. It could be that you talk too much—or too little—when I'm trying to say something. Maybe you leave me to flounder along as I try desperately to find words. Possibly I need to talk around and around something to find out where I am. Sometimes I know there is something inside me that I want to get out, but I'm not really zeroed in on what it is. Maybe I'm afraid of being rejected or of your thinking that what I say is trivial or silly. Instead of continuing to flounder—putting the burden on you to show patience and toleration—I should tell you about my frustration and ask for help.

You and I must honestly and openly talk over the effect of some of the things I say or the way I say them. Maybe my choice of words, tone of voice or pattern of speech turns you off. Maybe I won't allow myself to be touched or I won't touch you while I'm speaking, and that hurts. It could be that for me to believe I'm being listened to, I demand either explicitly or implicitly, agreement with my position. Maybe I'm just talking a lot and saying nothing. Or the opposite—I may talk very little, but when I do I expect instantaneous rapport, sympathy and understanding.

Overcoming these roadblocks to listening is something we must work on continually. If I'm not revealing myself on a regular basis, being open just one time will not be very effective. It's going to be almost impossible for you to fine-tune and hone in on me.

Maybe I allow my feelings to decide whether or not I'll listen to you. If I'm feeling close to you or there's a sense of warmth between us, then you're very important to me and everything you say counts. But if I'm wrapped up in my own thoughts and feeling down on myself—or you—or feeling lonely or isolated or tired, then I don't have any particular urgency to listen to you and I expect you to understand. With this kind of attitude, my listening becomes non-listening. Listening is determined not by where *I* am at any given moment, but where you are! The motivation for my listening should be *your* need, not mine. It's for what *you* get out of it.

My listening also could be determined by my feelings of being upset. Maybe something you say disturbs me, and I don't want to be disturbed so I tune you out. If you get rid of my hurt for me, then I'll listen. In other words, I'm making you decide what I'm willing to hear about you—I'm making you pay to have me listen. We excuse ourselves by saying, "What else can I do? Under the circumstances, I don't have any obligation to listen." Well, we must at least recognize that letting feelings determine our listening is not right; then there is some hope and possibility of change.

When we see that we can become effective listeners and that it isn't the other person who has to change, there will be a real desire on our part to improve.

What environment is best for listening?   *Your answer:*

When you feel a security and a closeness that enables you to be most yourself and to reveal whatever is going on inside you, then the setting is good for my listening!

So I need to consider listening important—important enough to prepare for it. I can't come home at night thinking of 75 other things, or greet you at the door and automatically assume that either of us is in a listening mood. We have to be thinking ahead of time, not just about what we're going to say to each other but how we're going to listen to each other.

Here are some helpful hints:

Listening usually occurs best when we're physically close to one another. Sitting side by side helps us to experience the presence of the other person and not just hear words.

Touching is important. We hear with our fingertips as well as with our ears.

Looking at each other helps us listen. We have to see into the other person and draw him or her inside us through our eyes. (We can learn a great deal about each other if we touch with our eyes as well as our hands!)

Considering how often and how spontaneously we listen well and how often we let our feelings or desires determine whether or not we listen can alert us to listening better.

Asking ourselves, "Do I consciously use the tools of listening I have at my disposal?" will help too. We can't program ourselves into being ready to listen whenever something big comes up. We have to practice on the smaller issues. We have to think ahead about what our particular strong points are and bring them into the foreground so that we can use them in the most effective way.

Looking at our defects and working to overcome them will increase our effectiveness.

With experience in listening the rewards will be great!

A "right" decision is not what is good for you or me but what is best for <u>us</u>.

2

Today I listed all the adventures we've talked about having!

DECISION-MAKING

**How would you rate
yourself as a
decision-maker?**

Your answer:

Let's look honestly at ourselves and make a fair evaluation of how
we see ourselves as decision-makers. After all, it's very important
in our lives to make decisions well. We all face situations in which
the decisions have a far-reaching significance. There are also
many little decisions we have to make every day. So the whole
process of decision-making plays a vital role in a couple's
marriage. We have to decide where we're going to live, what jobs
we're going to hold, and whether or not we will move with the job.
Should we have any of our in-laws live with us? How are we going

to spend our money? We also have the normal recurring decisions such as planning menus, or where we're going to spend the evening, or what we're going to do for a birthday or our anniversary or vacation.

We're like most couples if we don't give much thought to how we're making decisions. We just take it for granted that they have to be made and we do it. We do our best and complain later if things don't turn out well. We may be dissatisfied with some

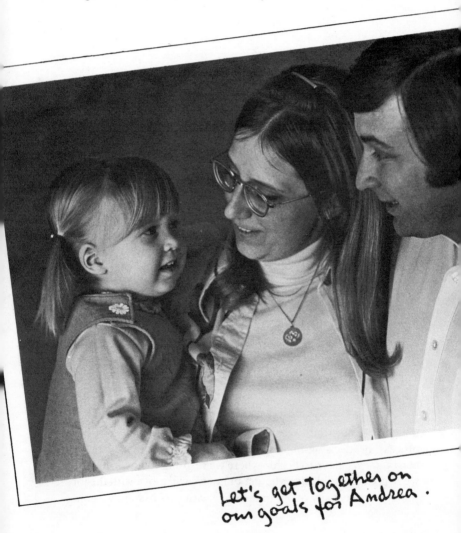

Let's get together on our goals for Andrea.

aspect of them, or feel pinched because we have so many to make, but we don't know what to do about it. Sometimes, of course, we fight with each other because we blame the other person for the way the decision turned out. We say things like, "I'm never going to let you make that decision again," or, "I won't follow your advice any more." Such a conclusion is not wise or prudent.

Decision-making is a main part of our lives, but we don't take classes on how to make decisions together. We probably never talk over *how* we should do it, what we see as good about the way we approach decisions together, what we see as needing some improvement, what we consider to be the basis of good decisions, what most interferes with our making good decisions. We could ask advice on how to make decisions or read articles to help us.

If we ignore this area or take it for granted that we're doing all right, we won't be living up to our potential. No matter what our talents may be, if we don't really look at our decision-making process and work to enrich it to the greatest possible degree, we're never going to be as good at it as we could be. We may agonize over decisions, looking at every angle and getting the best possible advice. But in all probability we don't look at *how* we approach making decisions. We just let it happen. That's not good enough. Part of the difficulty, of course, is that we're so distracted by the problem itself that we fail to see that the way we go about making the decision concerning it is sometimes even more important.

Why are your decisions consistently sound in some areas and not in others?   *Your answer:*

There are probably some situations we face in which our decisions are almost always good. We may not even realize how we make those decisions. But one of the best ways to go about improving the overall level of our decisions is to find out what we are doing right! How do we go about making the decisions which generally turn out well? If we can discover the qualities we exercise and the steps we take, we can apply them in the areas where our decisions are not turning out too well, or where we feel hesitant.

In all probability one of the fundamental reasons we make good decisions in a certain area is that this area is very important to us and we spend a lot of time and attention figuring out what would be the best choice to make. We become comfortable with all the different angles and situations that might come up. We believe we can cope with them and are not overwhelmed when a decision is needed. Familiar ground makes the difference.

We don't do well when we're hit by a new area. When we don't feel competent or knowledgeable, a situation calling for a decision floors us. We either withdraw from making a decision and postpone it until the last minute, or quickly make a judgment to get it over with so that we don't have to think about it any more. In both cases, it's a rash decision. Furthermore, we are predisposed to think poorly of ourselves.

Looking at the total problem helps us make better decisions. If a solution stands up over the long haul, we trust ourselves more the next time. It's sometimes easy to make a decision that solves an immediate problem but creates a bigger one for the future. A decision that solves a pressing need but doesn't take the future into account may be disastrous. For example, I might make a decision about my job that costs me longer hours and more tension. It solves the immediate problem of our need for money and helps pay our bills, but it puts a wedge in our marriage because I'm not around as much as I should be— or when I am around I'm so drained that I have nothing left to give to my wife.

Or, we could decide to have our children participate in dancing class or Little League or Scouts, which are good, but the activities take us away from each other because we're always driving the kids here, there and everywhere. We're seldom together. Our best decisions consider the long-term as well as the immediate effects.

And how about the decisions we make *together*? We gain a sense of solidarity, an awareness that we're not alone, that there's someone with whom to share the failures and the triumphs. We grow closer and experience joy in our oneness. We have injected the insights from both of us and considered the angles presented by each other, but the decision is our mutual responsibility.

What leads to difficulties in decision-making?

Your answer:

Making decisions is probably most difficult when we disagree on the goal. We can work out different ways to approach a common goal, but having different goals creates a major problem. Very often we don't know that our goals are different because we haven't talked about them. We know that we are not approaching the decision with one mind and one heart, but we don't know what to do about it. When a decision has to be made, we end up with some kind of compromise or surrender or grudging concession, and a non-involvement on the part of one or the other. That doesn't create an atmosphere in which decisions are made well or executed effectively.

What should we do to improve our way of making decisions when we have different goals? We have to take one step back and look at our values and where we are heading. Then we must work together to eliminate the differences, not in terms of browbeating each other or proving the other person right or wrong, but in honestly facing into each other to see the values behind the position the other person is taking. I need to honestly and sincerely experience your values and understand your goals.

That doesn't mean I have to adopt your position. But to be in harmony with each other in our decision-making, we will have to *share* each other's values—each of us understanding with the other's mind and heart.

The children's music had always been a source of conflict between Betty and Paul. Betty was very enthusiastic about lessons for all their children and although Paul wasn't flat against it he wasn't too much turned on by the idea. He saw that it was valuable and he was inclined toward it because Betty wanted it so much. But he wasn't eager to have the noise around the house in the evenings when he came home. Then they talked it out and found out that Betty had had lessons when she was a youngster and loved them. She very much wanted the children to have the same pleasure. It wasn't just that lessons were the right thing to do to develop their children's talents. As soon as Paul became aware of that, the situation changed for him. He started to take on some of what Betty was experiencing, so the decision to have music lessons for the children was an entirely different one. It was the two of them together wanting to share with their children the richness that she had experienced.

If our goals conflict in several areas of our lives, then the decisions we make are going to be, "I gave in the last time, so it's my turn to get my way this time." Or we'll end up just dividing areas of our life into individual responsibilities: this is hers and she makes the decisions here; that is his and he makes the decisions there. But that's giving up. It's surrender. It's saying that it's hopeless for us to get together, that we really can't work in harmony in this particular area, so just one will make the decision. Such an attitude may remove friction but it doesn't build our "coupleness."

In addition, our decisions are likely to be poor when we try to solve two problems at once. This happens when we are making one decision but have our eyes on another. We're not single-minded. We inject elements from the second problem into the first, thereby modifying the way we would approach the first problem if we were facing it by itself. This leads to confusion, especially if the concern for the second problem is in the mind of only one party!

Let's say a couple is deciding whether or not to get their son a bicycle. The wife knows that the son is not doing well in school and that when the father finds out, he will clamp down on the boy's privileges. She wants to get the boy that bike before the husband learns about the school situation, because once he knows, the bicycle is not going to happen. Another couple has to decide whether or not to buy a new car. The husband uses the decision for the car to get some promises from the wife to spend less money on the household. In both cases, the second issues should have been faced directly and not handled in a back-door fashion.

Our decisions are also apt to be poor when selfishness plays a large part—when I want my way, or I want something for myself and am determined to get it. That attitude leads us to make decisions we wouldn't make otherwise.

Such a decision has a snowball effect because it often leads the partner to retaliate. She says, "He got something for himself the last time, and now it's time for me to get my fair share." Or he might say, "Well, she's always getting her way, so I'm going to stand up for my rights."

We likewise have problems in the making of decisions if one or the other (or both of us) has more trust and more confidence in the advice and recommendations of other people than we do in each other. We should, of course, get advice and direction from others, but it can be an invigorating experience in oneness if we take that input and evaluate it together! All too often I present the advice from a friend, a counselor, a clergyman, or a business associate as Gospel and expect you to accept it. I have more faith in them than I do in you, and I'm letting a third party determine the way we live our lives. It isn't a question of whether or not their advice is sound. It may well be. But we have to live out the decision in *our* relationship, in *our* life pattern. The third party doesn't have to live it out at all! However good the advice may be in itself, it's really no good for us unless we use it to build our coupleness. It's in our relationship that a decision has to be made and executed.

There is also conflict in the making of decisions when one of us feels more capable and discredits the other. It's not that we believe there's anything stupid about our beloved, only that he or she is not informed enough on the particular subject or has not had enough experience.

For example, in deciding something regarding the children, the wife might think that her husband doesn't have enough exposure to them. She's with them all the time, so she believes her judgment is automatically better. Or when it comes to business or money, maybe the husband thinks his wife doesn't know what the business world is like or what the demands on the budget are. Therefore he doesn't accept the validity of her judgment regarding business or money.

When this trust factor is missing I may allow you to talk, and I may give you a certain amount of credibility, but I don't take you seriously. Consequently any decision that comes about is dissatisfying because you in effect have been excluded. When the next decision in that area is necessary you aren't eager to contribute anything because you know I won't let you become really involved. I put you on the defensive. You feel you have to prove you are reliable in this area, that you do have something valid to say. But as long as I have this prejudice against your capabilities, you are never going to be able to get through to me. I need to respect your opinion no matter what it is, so that we can make the decision together.

Another time when decision-making is weak is when one of us has an "I told you so" mentality. That drains confidence from the other person. It limits his freedom to reveal his thinking and to make recommendations. A person who's afraid of hearing "I told you so" is going to be cautious about getting involved in the decision. He's going to be unsure of himself. He's going to back away from it.

If we are to be fair to each other, we also have to give up the right to second-guess a decision. We might as well—it doesn't get either of us anyplace. This doesn't mean, of course, that we can't review a decision and see something we should have considered while making the decision or recognize a mistake we've made and see how to avoid a similar mistake in the future. When we do we take mutual responsibility for a decision gone awry. But if one of us stands off in innocence and points the finger at the other, that isn't good for either of us or for our relationship.

How frustrating it is to hear after the fact, "Y'know, I had a bad feeling about that decision," or, "I just had a sense in my gut that it wasn't going to work out right." Of course the speaker never mentioned it at the time! It can drive the other person up the wall. He might say, "Well, why didn't you say so?"

"Well," comes the reply, "You seemed so certain, and I didn't want to throw a monkey wrench into things. Besides, you're always asking my reasons for being hesitant about something, and I couldn't give you any reason, so I just didn't tell you what my sense of the thing was."

What we're doing is claiming credit for having had the right instinct, even though we didn't reveal it to our spouse at the time, and telling him that it was his fault that we didn't bring it out. So we have the best of two worlds. We were nice guys in going along on the decision and being very considerate of our spouse, and at the same time we were right all along!

Our decision-making is also likely to go badly when one of us insists on a decision because of some kind of mysterious instinct or "experience radar." I don't give you any reasons to chew on or any research to cope with. I just say, "Trust me." "My intuition tells me this," or, "My experience leads me to take this stand." However, intuition and instinct—the gut feelings—come from past experiences, how we saw other people react under similar conditions or how we ourselves reacted and what that led us to believe. They are not mysterious things at all. Both are based on evidence. They're not logical reasons, but they are reasonable. They can be explained.

I can't in fairness give you a conclusion without sharing what led me to it.

Which of you usually makes the decisions?

Your answer:

It sometimes happens in a couple relationship that one person, either the husband or the wife, consciously or unconsciously falls into the role of decision-maker. Both may have agreed that one of them is the more levelheaded of the two. Therefore when a problem comes up the "decision-maker" formulates a judgment. It's expedient. The husband and wife are more interested in getting the decision made than in making the decision as a couple. This has a debilitating effect on the relationship; it practically eliminates one party from any responsibility for the decision. He can throw in his ideas, but he doesn't take the importance of the decision seriously because he senses that the decision-maker is going to have the final say anyway. The couple may not actually be aware of what's happening.

This can be a little bit sticky when both husband and wife believe as Jay and Cynthia did that because they talked it over together the two of them had a mutual say in the decision.

However, although Cynthia reasoned out each step of the decision to its logical conclusion, it was Jay who took the final step and announced the decision. The whole thing had been set up by Cynthia! Neither of them realized it. So even though it appeared that they shared equally in the decision, they did not.

It's easy enough to kid ourselves on who is making the decision, because we sometimes think, "I don't always get my way," or, "Very frequently I give in to him," or, "I often let her have what she wants." But who arrives at the conclusion that I've given in to him or that she has been satisfied? If I do, then I am still making the decision.

Do each of you have your decision-making areas?

Your answer:

Sometimes by discussion, sometimes by assumption, sometimes by accident, a couple assign specific areas of their lives to one or the other for making decisions. It might be that decisions of the home are the wife's and decisions about finances are the husband's, neither seeing anything wrong with that arrangement. They are quite content to live that way.

It can seem very reasonable. After all, there are many decisions to be made, and whoever has the most competence or the most experience or faces the decisions most frequently is the expert. It can look as though each person is placing his trust in the other for his assigned area. Each knows the other is considerate, won't take advantage, and will be understanding of his needs. Furthermore, it doesn't mean a decision is made without consulting the other. A great deal of thought may have been given to what each person wants. A lot of discussion may have centered around what each thinks. But both recognize that when it comes down to actually making the final decision, the partner who is the decider in that area has his way.

Unfortunately, the party who is not the decision-maker is simply an interested observer or a consultant. When it comes to the children, the husband is at best no more than a shoulder to lean upon or a sounding board off which to bounce ideas; he doesn't get involved. Ultimately the wife is going to make the decisions herself. As far as finances are concerned, the wife, knowing the husband is generous and, in fact, will take her needs more into consideration than his own, doesn't have to get involved.

The point is not whether the decisions are better than the ones they would make together. The point is that a one-party decision does not advance the couple's relationship. It might advance the finances and the education or discipline of the children, but it's not a real part of their marriage.

Many wives concede, "He's so much better at this! He knows much more than I do. I'm only a housewife." And husbands say, "She manages the children so smoothly! I'm not around that much. It's really better if she makes the home decisions."

The net result is, of course, that the total burden of finances or of the children is put on one party. It's entirely up to the one partner to assume that responsibility and to make the correct decisions. He not only has the burden by himself, but he also has to answer to his spouse for the correctness of his decisions. The spouse may be very generous and not say, "I told you so," yet feels absolved from any personal participation.

Now what do they have? A rather spotty marriage. In whole areas of their married life they are not involved with each other. It is a living-out of the mentality that says marriage is a partnership rather than a call to unity. It makes us task-oriented. The way we handle our tasks determines our goodness. That's a poor basis. So instead of being "efficient," it's better to become more aware of each other and more integrated into each other's lives.

Most husbands try to provide as good a living for their families as possible. They recognize that they have to help out with the kids and do odd jobs around the house. Most wives are wonderful about taking care of the house, being good mothers to the children, having good meals on time when their husbands come home from work.

Anne and Ray did very well by one another, but still there was a nagging dissatisfaction in both of them. They talked more and

more about what they were experiencing inside themselves and how they were anxious for even a better life together. They knew that it wasn't going to be accomplished by having more things, or by his getting a promotion at his job or by her keeping the house better. They recognized that while each appreciated everything the other person did for him, they were looking for more opportunity to talk to each other, a greater sense of being listened to and understood.

Anne began to realize that when Ray came home from work she was in full gear getting meals ready, making sure that the kids were doing their homework and getting off to bed, and she really wasn't conscious of him. She was grateful that he was home and that he could take some of the burden of the children off her, but he was an assistant baby sitter. She recognized that she had to gear down and *do* less in order to *be* more for him. She began to prepare herself mentally for his coming home and deliberately and consciously chose to have time with him.

Ray realized pretty much the same thing, that he was caring about getting ahead in his job so that he could provide better for the family. The more they talked, the more he saw that providing for Anne was much more personal than his paycheck. It wasn't the *things* that he was able to offer her that made him valuable in her life. It was *he* who was valuable to her.

Maybe they don't score as high now in their husband-and-wife roles, but there's a sparkle in her eye and a lightness in his step when he comes home at night. Now they really enjoy each other's company!

The most important factor in any decision is *the effect it has on our relationship*. Decisions made solely on the basis of who has the most knowledge or the most experience will not improve it. The focus of such decision-making is away from each other rather than toward each other.

A bad decision made together is not necessarily going to bring us closer to each other, but maybe the decision that makes less business sense or Dr. Spock sense is the better one for us—especially in the long run. After all, the whole point of earning money is to allow us to live more meaningfully with each other; the whole point of raising children is for us to be present as a couple to our children, teaching them to become lovers.

We can make all kinds of right decisions regarding the children, but the effectiveness of the decisions is minimized if we do not communicate the warmth of our relationship. The highest motivation for children is not that a decision makes sense or that it's the best possible thing to do under the existing conditions, but rather that it means something to *us*. If it means something to only one of us, it's deficient. If we make decisions together, everything we do will be more effective—both for our couple relationship and for our children.

Which of you comes to decisions more quickly, and what effect does that have?

Your answer:

It's usual in interpersonal relationships for one person to be quicker and more decisive than the other. It doesn't necessarily mean that one is slow; it just means that one is faster.

One result is that the decisions are made by the quicker decision-maker in his acceptance or rejection of the recommendation. In other words, if I'm the quicker one, I signal my decision and we end up choosing my way of doing things. We don't really decide together. I may be open to your suggestions and I may be willing to change, but it's *my* plan that's on the line between us and you never get a chance.

The quicker decision-maker might try to improve the situation by saying to himself, "I will hold back so she will have an opportunity to come up with a plan." That's an improvement that the quicker one should definitely consider, but there's an even

Slo-o-o-w down. I need more time to figure this out.

better way to treat the situation. I, as the faster decision-maker, will slow down in the very formulation of our position, so that we consciously take each step together. Otherwise I will have had more time to come to grips with my decision; I'll be able to back it with more arguments; I'll have seen more of the possible objections to it and will have plugged up the loopholes; I'll be at an advantage when we start talking over the plan, even if I let you have your say first.

Because the quicker decision-maker is always at an advantage and his direction is usually adopted, the slower person tends to become even slower, maybe even gives up. He figures he can never catch up anyway—he might as well wait until a decision is presented to him before he reacts. In that case the couple doesn't get each other's input. They just get the objections or the approval of what the quicker one has decided.

65

Do you control each other in the way you make decisions?

Your answer:

We can influence—or force—the other person to make a decision by our rate of speed. For example, a fast person may come up with one solution after another and force the other person to take one or another of what is offered. The slower one may initially turn down all of them, but after a while feel that he's been too negative by saying no, no, no. So he says yes just because so many solutions are presented.

He can also be pushed into making a decision before he's ready because the faster person comes across with strength and urgency. Besides, it's embarrassing to offer no solutions while the other person has 17 per square inch.

On the other hand, a slow person can also exert pressure. He can give the impression that he is reliable, thoughtful, and more to be trusted in making decisions, thus implying that the other person is rash or inexact.

The ponderous person can be so slow-moving—examining every little detail, questioning every facet and every line of approach—that he frustrates the other party to pieces. The spouse will be willing to accept any decision just to get a decision made. He'll throw up his hands and say, "Do anything you want, just do something!"

A slow person can even put the blame on the partner when things go wrong and say, "Because you rushed so, you made me come to a decision when I wasn't ready for it—I didn't have time to think it through." The implication is that in the future the other person should accept the slower person's way of doing things.

Sometimes we play these games with each other without being aware of what we're doing. And the problems are compounded when we assign different areas of decisions according to the rate of speed called for. One can take those that call for slow decisions—the other can take those that need quick decisions.

It's better that there be a commitment by both spouses to get involved in the overall decision-making process.

We have to develop a "couple pace" of making decisions rather than maintaining our individual paces. The slow person can learn to go a bit faster, and the faster one can learn to slow down. The point is somehow to formulate our decisions together. We want to approach the various situations as a couple.

Sheila found it very easy to make decisions that affected the running of the household and couldn't understand why Lonny was so slow. He was slow because he was always asking how much it cost. On the other hand, he was always volunteering them for outside activities and getting them involved in organizations. He made those decisions right away. Sheila couldn't respond quickly here. She wanted to know what she was getting into and how much of her time it was going to take up. They gradually realized that the one who was slow in a given area was slow because he was most affected.

Lonny hesitated on household decisions because of the budget. Sheila hesitated on outside obligations because of the family demands on her time. When they had a clearer idea of what the consequences were of the choice they were making, they listened to each other better. They didn't have such a sense of being impeded or slowed down or interfered with. There wasn't the frustration they'd had. Their decisions became cooperative. They were no longer two people standing on opposite sides.

Of course, we may differ in other ways in our decision-making. For example, one of us might be sharp, clear, definitive and decisive. The other one might be cautious, gentle, investigative, option-oriented. Each of these qualities is good and has definite advantages. But if we maintain our individual qualities and don't mesh ours with our spouse's, every difficulty imaginable can occur. We may use these good qualities to control each other or to get our way. Or we may divide the decision-making areas according to what best matches the qualities of each of us, rather than working out decisions together.

Here's another difference: one party likes to talk out a decision, and the other likes to think about it, working it completely through in his mind first. The one works it out with his mind before he proposes it to his spouse, presents a "take it or leave it" situation. He isn't cruel about it; he may be perfectly willing to accept a "leave it" from his spouse and rethink the problem. But still he's formulating a decision on his own. Even though he's considering the other person, it's his decision.

To have a couple decision we have to cover the complete process together, from the gathering of the data, through each step, considering our values, taking into account the speed with which we think and decide our goals, all the way to the execution of the decision. More important than anything else in our decision-making is that we be comfortable with *each other* and aware of *each other* every step of the way.

Which of you is the better decision-maker and what effect does that have?

Your answer:

If you have a superior talent in making decisions, it's part of your contribution to your marriage. It's a gift you bring to your spouse, a skill that profits both of you. However, there are several road signs advising caution. Be sure your skill is real, not just a reputed one.

It may appear that you do better than your spouse at making decisions because you are quicker and more decisive than he, or because you are more thoughtful and seem to reason things out more fully. But being fast or slow does not in itself make for good decisions.

Sometimes we think a lot of education makes a person more competent in decision-making. That is not necessarily true either. A person who has very little education—or less than his spouse—may be a much better decider.

If one party definitely has a skill in making choices, the skill must still be at the service of both. Consider the wife who has a great ability to cook. The talent is to a large degree wasted if she cooks so that she alone can enjoy the food or get a sense of satisfaction from having cooked well. The talent serves when it is used for his sake too, and for the sake of their relationship.

A man may have a great ability to make money, and do well in business, but that may have little to do with his relationship with his wife. The skill or talent we have, including decision-making, must be used with our beloved, for his sake and for the sake of our relationship.

Are there hindrances to making good decisions?

Your answer:

During the day many decisions come up that have to be made immediately. Most of them are *patterned decisions,* ones in which we know what our spouse thinks. Other decisions we can foresee. They can be talked over ahead of time. Then your thinking can be clearly in my mind when I'm making that decision. Frictions in a marital relationship occur when a husband or wife is often making decisions and afterward finding out they upset the other person.

We tend to excuse ourselves when we do this, saying, "I was really trying; I had the best intentions in the world. I just didn't know." But we really can't excuse ourselves for not knowing. If we could reasonably have anticiapted that this type of decision was going to come up in the immediate future, we should have talked it over ahead of time.

Because making couple decisions is a new thing, a developing thing, for marrieds, the process isn't without problems. Maybe one person always takes the initiative. It would be good for him to hold back once in a while and deliberately let his spouse come in first with ideas.

Of course, a lot of times the more reticent person likes it better when the stronger one takes the initiative, because then he has a chance to counterpunch. He can pick the decision apart and come in with his own solution. We have to examine ourselves to see if we're controlling each other by the way we approach a decision.

Sometimes we don't make decisions because we leave them till the last minute. Of course, none of us really likes decisions. It's so much responsibility! If we make a mistake, we have to pay a price. If we planned ahead, one good, solid, well-thought-out decision could take the place of ten scattered little ones. Lots of times those ten little ones end up being bad because we make them under the pressure of having to come up with instant solutions.

Because a decision often has all kinds of implications—a sort of ripple effect—we have to consider every angle. Only then can we see whether one decision would be more reasonable than another. For example, to have a better home a couple may decide to move to a suburb. It means the husband has to drive an hour and a half to work every day. Consequently the wife will have more responsibility and have to make many decisions on her own regarding the children, and she will be lonely.

Also, the two of them will be less involved in their marriage. They don't mean that to happen. The decision was meant to be for the good of their marriage. So, when he is home, he will have to make an extraordinary effort to pay attention to his wife. And she will have to become quite independent or she will demand too much when he is home.

Another consequence may involve deciding about a second car, which they may or may not want to do at the time they buy the house. Furthermore, they're putting themselves at the mercy of leases and mortgages, which may necessitate a decision some-where down the pike about whether or not the wife goes back to work. Also, moving may mean a split-off from their families. Their parents may now have to stay overnight, whereas before they just came for an afternoon. Maybe the couple will have to make new decisions about their social life because the husband has to get up much earlier than before to get into town—he just can't take those late hours.

Nothing is wrong with any of the decisions that have to be made. But it's better that they not come as a surprise! Had a couple thought about the implications ahead of time the decisions would have been easier to make, or maybe the original decision about the house would never have been made!

Though one decision may be closely related to another, we often look at them separately, analyzing each one in terms of what is best at this particular time, the most sensible answer to this kind of problem. Such an approach may allow us to make good individual decisions that are perfectly defensible in themselves, but it can lead us to mess up our whole way of life or our vision of what we're all about as a couple. We need to integrate our decisions into an overall plan. But we often don't take time to do it because we think we can beat the odds. We look at our individual circumstances, and we figure no matter what happens to everyone else when they make the same type of decision, it's not going to happen to us.

We've figured it all out together, so New Orleans, here we come!

For example, we look at the suburban mentality and read all sorts of newspaper articles and books about it. We know about the isolation and loneliness of the "nuclear family," the one in which there is just husband, wife and children, with no extended family of uncles, aunts or grandparents. We go ahead and make a decision in terms of immediate satisfaction or freedom, without facing the fact that we're just as human as anyone else. We can—and probably will—fall into the very same difficulties as others do. Very few of us beat the system while playing the system's games. We would have to get completely away from the system if we were to really live our own lives. Because we don't break away, we end up making the same decisions as anyone else. Actually, we've set up circumstances whereby we have almost no freedom in our decisions at all.

We honestly believe we are independent. Yet we end up being Bobbsey twins to our neighbors. We have to develop freedom of choice for ourselves, taking into account all the implications.

Carl finally got the promotion with a good, hefty raise in pay that he and Alice had been waiting for. When he burst into the house, he was so full of his joy that he didn't have to tell her. Alice just said, "You got it! You got it!" They reveled in their good fortune for several days and then they began to plan. Up until this time Alice had worked because it was necessary in order to keep their heads above water. Alice's job gave her a sense of independence and importance, and now the money she earned there could go for some of the luxuries they hadn't been able to afford. On the other hand, she'd always dreamed of going back to school to get her degree. She'd always wanted to be a college graduate for her own dignity and sense of self-worth. Besides, it would qualify her for an even better job. They had a lot of fun talking over the different advantages of each possibility. One day they mentioned it to a dear friend whose advice they respected and trusted. He said to them, "I don't think you're considering all the options. You're just taking the most obvious ones. Isn't it possible that neither the job nor school is the best choice for you? At least consider the idea of taking the freedom that you've now been granted, quitting the job, and not going back to school—just being total in the time and attention that you spend on your marriage. Don't fall into the trap of thinking that just because more money or education is good for one of you, it's good for both of you."

Bob and Alice weren't particularly sold on the idea, but they decided that it couldn't hurt them to talk about it. Bob said, "Y'know Alice, it is true that the way I've been thinking is that if you're happy and content you'll be less uptight, less frustrated, and automatically my life will be better."

Alice responded, "We've been just thinking about me. We really haven't been thinking about us—both of us together. You and I have been looking for something outside of us to provide our satisfaction in life."

"That's true. I haven't really expected you to satisfy me. I've been filling my life with my job and not with you, instead of the other way around."

"What it really comes down to, I guess, is that I really didn't think that our marriage was that important. Or to be even more honest about it, I didn't really believe that I was worth your full time and attention, that I could really satisfy you. I guess I was afraid to be the center of your life because then I would have to make you the center of mine."

Alice and Bob admitted to each other that they were scared. It was risky to count that much on each other. But they made the decision not only to do it this time, but to make it their general norm to decide everything on how it affected the *two* of them rather than how it affected either of them as individuals.

Do you constantly redo decisions?

Your answer:

We may make decisions and act on them, but in our minds we may still not be committed to them. In that case, we keep second-guessing ourselves and our spouse and want to reopen the questions all the time. The decisions are never really settled. This is very debilitating and draining in a relationship because it doesn't give us any peace. We're doing double duty—dealing with old decisions over again as well as facing new ones! It gets to be a constant hassle. It also leads to a lack of confidence in ourselves. When we go into a decision, we know it will take a long, long time to hash out. We know we're never going to be at peace with it anyway, so we tend to avoid the whole thing. We run away from making any decisions because they're painful. We're killing ourselves by not finalizing anything!

First of all, we need to be honest with ourselves and ask: Are we redoing decisions because we didn't spend enough time on them in the first place? Are we checking out decisions after they have been made rather than beforehand?

Another reason for lack of finality may be that we made the decision but one person or the other, though he agreed externally, wasn't at peace with it. Or maybe neither of us was satisfied with it. The decision keeps popping up again in one of these forms: "I told you so" or, "Are you really sure?" or, "Do you think we ought to look at this thing again because, after all, it's so serious?"—and on and on.

On the other hand I may inject something as if it were a new angle, but actually I'm showing that I don't have any confidence in your decision-making powers. I'm attacking your self-confidence. Of course something may well come up we didn't know about beforehand, but at some point we have to put the decision to rest.

Any decision could be wrong. There's no guarantee a decision is automatically going to be right. We should look at each of our decisions and come to a common agreement. Then we should live with that decision. It's not that we never change our minds. But we want to avoid constantly reassessing everything.

Do you have hidden agendas in your decision-making?

Your answer:

We're often guilty of deceiving ourselves in decision-making. We don't face what's honestly in our minds. We use symbols. I may be shy and nervous about bringing up a certain subject, so I go into

Let's get together — once and for all.

another that is close to it but not as touchy. We make a decision on a certain topic, but in my mind something else is behind it. For example, in making a decision on allowances for the children, I try to see whether you're open enough for me to push for some of the things I want. Or, the decision to be made may be on where we're going to go this evening, but the question underneath is, "Do we go to your friends or my friends?"

We aren't honestly facing into one another and what is standing between us. We're skirting the topic, the *real* topic. We don't come to grips with the real issue. The horror that's involved here lies in the assumptions and interpretations we make. We assume that we know the other person's position on the second topic by what he's saying about the first. Because the husband wants to give minimal allowances to the children, the wife assumes he's upset with the way she's spending money or that he's not open to their talking about a change in spending habits. The wife may want to visit some of her friends, so the husband assumes that she doesn't like his friends. In such a situation, a couple needs to decide between them how the friends of each fit into their lives and which ones are going to become their *mutual* friends. Unless they begin thinking and talking on the "couple" level, they'll never come to an understanding of each other.

One of the big tip-offs to this problem is the times we are just not in harmony with each other, and can't seem to get anything across. The other person seems to misunderstand whatever we say. Sure, we could be in a bad mood or not be clear in what we're saying, but the most likely reason is a hidden agenda. We need to bring into the open exactly what concerns us and discuss it.

Joe and Martha were sitting around talking one evening and Joe brought up the subject of the family vacation. It was a little bit early. It was still March and his vacation wasn't until August but vacations had always meant a lot to them. It was always exciting to anticipate them. But the conversation didn't go well.

It seemed to Joe that Martha was negative. Every place he brought up to visit in their camper, she was against. He found himself getting irritated and frustrated. He thought he was being very accommodating. If she didn't like going North, well then, he was willing to go South. But she didn't like the South either, so he tried the East and West, and neither of them was satisfactory.

He found himself arguing, trying to force her to agree. Finally he wanted to throw up his hands and say they'd stay home. But something stopped him and as gently and understandingly as he could he said, "Martha, what's really the matter? I know that this is not like you. Let's get it out and talk about it."

"It's never any vacation for me," Martha said. "It's only more work for me." That really set Joe back. He hadn't even thought about that. He realized he hadn't really pitched in to make it a vacation for her too.

They started to talk about that part of it. They decided to shorten their vacation by a couple of days so that they could go out to eat more often. She wouldn't have to do so much cooking and cleaning up. Once they had faced into the real difficulty, they could talk about their vacation again.

Unrelated issues, often raised because he vetoed the new washing machine or she said no the night before, are brought up as a smoke screen to even things off with the other person or to give vent to frustration. Many times we don't even know we're being unreasonable. We just feel out of sorts. We're upset because of something the other person has done. We pick a subject or approach a decision in a way we know will upset or annoy the other person.

Do you consider feelings in making decisions?   *Your answer:*

An important part of any human being is his feelings. They should be a part of the input in any decision. Maybe "X" number of dollars is an adequate amount of money for Ruth to have each week for groceries, but she may get so upset about having to count the pennies that Jerry has to give her "Y" number of dollars. Maybe they should visit Ruth's mother a particular day, but Jerry is so tense and uptight that he knows he's going to be miserable if he does.

We need to take each other's feelings into account when we're approaching a decision. If we don't, we may make a decision that is not good for us, even though it's correct.

We have to talk not primarily about what our position is but about how each decision makes us feel. What's going on inside of us—the feelings stirred up by the thought of that decision—is a factor in making a decision.

It doesn't mean the decisions are based on feelings. However, feelings are part of the information both of us need to have in order to come to an intelligent and prudent decision between us. Because feelings are not always faced, one or both of us may be unable to live with a decision.

Maybe Helen and Fred are looking at a decision that would call for them to scrimp and save for several years. After that they would be in very good shape financially. But what if the scrimping and saving would cause them so much upset and frustration it would destroy their marriage? Their feelings need to be anticipated.

It doesn't have to be as serious as that. It may be merely that one or the other of us will wind up being uncomfortable with a decision, so we have to talk about it. Discussing it doesn't necessarily mean that we're going to change the decision, However, we may add or subtract something in order to handle the uncomfortableness.

If feelings are not considered in our decisions, we'll get a whiplash from them. Most of us are not immune to feelings. It's how we feel on any given day that determines how we look at life and each other. Decisions we make together taking our feelings into account will have a good chance of being successful.

Grace looked forward to the evenings she and Matt went out for dinner with their friends. They always had such a good time! Matt was a bit out of sorts sometimes, but Grace reassured herself that that's the way men were. One night when she was putting the finishing touches to her hair and humming happily, Matt made more of a scene than usual. Finally she said to him, "Look, why do you have to spoil it for me? Why can't we just have a nice evening out together as a couple?"

"That's exactly it," said Matt. "We're not a couple. It's your thing. I'm nothing. I feel very lonely on nights like this. I'm just along for the ride. I'm the chauffeur. I'm part of the scenery. I never have any say in where we're going or what we're doing. I'm just told where we're going to go. What do you think that makes me feel like? Well, c'mon, that's the way it's going to be, so let's go."

It wasn't a very pleasant evening for either of them. Grace was angry at first for having her night ruined, but before she went to sleep and the next day she thought about what Matt had said. She began to understand how he felt.

When he came home from work she said, "Y'know, you're right. From here on in, let's talk together about how each of us feels concerning where we're going and what we're going to do and with whom we're going to spend our time. It's not true that you're just a part of the scenery. I do want to be with you but I haven't shown that. Thanks for waking me up."

Are your decisions based on feelings?   *Your answer:*

Most of us tend to make decisions in terms of how we feel. We're likely to do what attracts us. We're not likely to do what turns us off. We don't like to admit it, but that's what we do. We try to convince ourselves that we're deciding things on worthy principles or good sound reasoning. But actually even the impulse to discover reasons results from the way we feel. Maybe the basic feeling underlying a decision is my loneliness. So I figure out all sorts of reasons to support taking a job or getting involved in some activity or looking for more attention from my spouse. I say we need more income, we should help more in the community or we should think about the house more. These reasons may be good and valid, but the motivating factor is my loneliness.

Maybe I have enthusiasm for a hobby or buying something that costs a great deal of money, so I work out all sorts of logical reasons for going ahead. Without that enthusiasm, though, I would not have been interested enough to discover those reasons.They alone would not have motivated me to take on the hobby or pay for the possession.

The problem with making decisions based on feelings is that feelings change. They often don't last from moment to moment, much less from day to day or week to week. My loneliness may dissipate, my enthusiasm may evaporate—or it may intensify. If I base my decisions on feelings, I'm standing on sand.

Sound values, good reasoning, fundamental principles, do last. If we make decisions based on them, our decisions will be consistent, and we know where we are with each other. If we base decisions on feelings, we never really know where we are with ourselves or each other.

This is not a contradiction of what was said previously about feelings. Feelings have to be part of our knowledge in making a decision, but they shouldn't be the determining factor. If they are, we will be constantly changing the decision to match our moods and feelings!

For example, it's easy to be nice to each other when we *feel* "nice." And it's easy to be distant from or careless toward each other when we're not feeling particularly warm or close. So our relationship is often based on our feelings—which are uncertain guides to say the least. When we're not feeling nice, we think up all sorts of reasons to explain why we're unpleasant, and many of the reasons are attacks on the other person. When we're feeling fine and being pleasant toward each other, we don't work out reasons, because who needs a reason for feeling good?

When we're under the heavy pressure of enthusiasm or insecurity or any other feeling, we would do well to postpone the decision and wait until we're in control of ourselves—until we're capable of making the decision with our heads instead of with our stomachs.

It helps to analyze some of our previous decisions so that we can recognize how large a part feelings have played in them. When we see what has worked out and what hasn't, we can make better decisions next time.

Furthermore, we have to talk to each other about our feelings.

If I don't recognize that my feelings play a large part in my decision-making, my spouse might. He can help me be honest with myself. This is a wonderful thing about husbands and wives. They can help each other overcome the self-delusion with which we are all afflicted. It would be a serious mistake to believe we can come to grips with our self-delusions by ourselves, especially in the area of feelings. We're so used to making decisions according to our feelings that it's hard for us to recognize when it's happening. But together couples can do it and build a stronger basis for their choices.

Do you consider it important to make your decisions as a couple?

Your answer:

The whole question of decision-making is based not simply on whether a couple makes sound decisions with good results. Unless they're making decisions as a couple, they might as well not be married.

Marriage is a way of life based on the decisions we make to commit ourselves to each other and to live out that commitment on a daily basis. If the decisions are made by two individuals who simply happen to live together or have certain vested interests in each other, they do not have a marriage. They have a roommate situation—which is one of the reasons so many couples experience dissatisfaction and loneliness. They are not able to achieve the hopes and dreams they had when they were first married.

A couple decision has as its common stake the two of them and their relationship. It is one in which the husband and wife come together with whatever their approaches are—they may be different—and meld into one another and come out with a decision based on their oneness. They're not simply agreeing on a decision, they are discovering it together. It isn't that they have met at the point of the decision, but rather that the two of them have gone through the whole process together.

The motivation behind the decision is not what is best for you or me, but what is best for *us*. Naturally, something that is best for you is a plus factor for me because of the spillover effect on our relationship; but if the decision is reached in terms of what is best for us, it will also be best for you and me. We approach decisions as two individuals who have a mutual interest in the decision not for itself, but for the advancement of our relationship. Our coupleness is our main concern.

The focus of marriage is for us to become two in one flesh, to become united with each other. We should not lose our individuality or our personalities—it takes two "I's" to make one "we"— but we should deliberately focus on our becoming a "couple" unit. A very good way to strengthen our oneness is to make decisions together. When we dare to get into it all the way, we'll find a new kind of adventure that makes marriage more exciting than ever.

We're much more than roommates!

The point of ... fighting —
is to get closer to each other.

3

FIGHTING

Do you pride yourselves on never or hardly ever fighting?

Your answer:

Whenever couples start talking about their marriages, the issue of fighting is raised, usually in kidding terms. Everybody smiles knowingly, taking it for granted that everyone knows what husband-and-wife fighting is all about. And in the undercurrent there is an unspoken conviction that fighting is inevitable in marriage, that everybody does it, that it is one of the prices you pay for being married.

And yet, in any group, a couple is likely to say, or at least feel, "We're not like that. We never fight." Or, "We used to be that way, but we've grown out of it." Sometimes couples use their not fighting as evidence that their marriage is a good one. They'll say, "In 25 years we haven't had a single fight!" Listeners react with wonder or disbelief. They may think the couple is fighting secretly, or take the statement as it stands and agree that it is evidence that the couple has a good marriage.

Wait a minute. Let's ask ourselves: "Does an absence of fights indicate a good marriage?" It would be easy to think so. After all, nobody likes to fight; the hurt and pain that come from fighting are severe and leave scars. The pain can also reduce the communication between husband and wife. Without a doubt there are advantages to not fighting. The sharp active hurts are not present in a no-fight relationship. There is a lot of goodness in that couple; they've learned to bite their tongues, to discipline themselves. They avoid a lot of turmoil.

All that is good. But what price do they pay? They are less involved with each other! They have suppressed their thoughts and feelings. They have lost their openness and honesty with each other. They have swallowed hard and walked away from each other. The result in the long run, with years of practice, is that they don't have to swallow quite so hard; they don't have to walk away quite so far, and they're not quite so easily upset as at first. They have paid a very high cost for not fighting. They've trained themselves not to be emotionally involved. That is not good. In fact, the price they're paying is higher than the reward they're getting. They have bought this kind of calmness, this lack of turmoil, at the price of a close relationship. No one can afford it.

Though it's a very attractive temptation, "peace at any price" is not a good idea. Couples learn not to say things that might rock the boat; they avoid touchy areas. Their relationship is not a full one. It's one in which certain subjects are not gone into with any depth or never gone into at all. It means the couple have to always be in control. They can never let their guard down. They have to train themselves not to notice each other very much. That way they won't get disturbed. If they get bothered they have to pretend it's not important. It means keeping whole areas of their lives separate so that she has her responsibilities and he has his. That way they don't rub up against each other very frequently; they are less likely to rub each other the wrong way.

In such a situation we're concentrating on what we're *not* doing rather than on what we can do. To get close to each other entails the risk of upsetting the other person or getting hurt oneself. Unless that risk is taken, we're living in a roommate situation in which we get along and have a certain compatibility and a fine cooperative spirit, but we're not involved with each other. The probing that's necessary for deep revelaton will on occasion generate frictions which could mushroom into fights. The only way fights can be avoided over an extended period of time is through non-involvement; yet involvement is what a couple is for!

Do you pride yourself on not starting fights?   *Your answer:*

In any husband-and-wife relationship, one party is usually more likely to start the fights than the other. One spouse is the more apt to blow up and the other tends to be more placid, at least until stirred up into some kind of reaction. The personality of the individuals or the choice of topic may determine who starts the fight.

Because of the mentality which says a good marriage is proven by the absence or scarcity of fights over a period of years, the one who doesn't start the fights tends to look on himself as virtuous. He credits himself with not being to blame, no matter how severely he might attack once the fight has started. He takes credit for having poured oil on troubled waters for whatever length of time they've not had a fight, and he throws up his hands in disgust that the other person can't control himself. He looks on his spouse as too volatile, too emotional, too easily upset, or too sensitive.

But it isn't that simple. I have to take an honest look at why it is that I never seem to start the fights. Maybe the reason is negative. Maybe I don't care much what happens. I'm not involved, so things don't really get to me. I'm more interested in my children or job or shrubs. I can take everything else in stride.

Maybe my spouse is concerned with what is going on between us and the only way to get me to talk and reveal what is going on inside me is to start a fight. It's only when I'm under the heavy pressure of being attacked that I speak up and show myself. Maybe I've put up such a mask of perfection—acting the cool, calm and collected type—that it takes a sledge hammer to get through to me.

Possibly, too, a fight is the only way to get me to *listen*. Maybe I just chatter away gaily or philosophize volubly and never give my spouse a chance to get a word in edgewise. The only way to get me to stand still is to derail me. It's painful for both of us, but maybe the experience of our years together proves it's the only thing that works.

Or maybe I'm the type of person who lives in a dream world, thinking everything is going along okay all the time. I don't have much sensitivity; my antennae aren't finely tuned. The only way to impress on me that everything *isn't* okay between us is to shout. I may, in other words, be hard of hearing when it comes to how badly we're doing together. Maybe my beloved has to start a fight in order to have any part in my life!

Do you provoke fights even if you don't start them?   *Your answer:*

Fights don't start at the moment of the first angry word. Fights are started by the atmosphere created by some situation. If a magnifying glass is held over a pile of straw in the noonday sun, sooner or later that straw is going to start smoldering. But the magnifying glass didn't start the fire, the circumstances did. So the person who seems to start the fight may not be responsible for it. The other person may have created the atmosphere in which a

C'mon, let's talk about what's really bothering you.

fight was inevitable. He stands back in perfect innocence when the other person explodes. For example, a wife might finally blow up in desperation after a whole evening of heavy silence from her husband. A man who has had constant interruptions by his wife while he has been trying to get the income tax done might finally hit the ceiling.

There are many ways we can provoke fights. We do things we know will upset the other person; we open up a touchy subject; we go into a weighty subject at an inappropriate time. We pick away at the other person with all sorts of little requests or with seventeen and a half different complaints per half hour. We communicate in non-verbal ways, saying we're upset at the other person but won't talk about it. We're constantly absorbed in doing our own thing or satisfying our own interests, and we don't pay attention to the other person, so the only way he can get us back into focus is by creating a scene.

One of the most "magnificent" ways of provoking a fight is to play the martyr's role—letting the other person know, in either subtle or not-so-subtle ways, how much of a burden we're carrying, how heroic we are, what sacrifices we're making. Sometimes martyrdom can be a way of crucifying the other person.

Another way to start a fight is to continually forget little things that are important to the other person. We seem unable to remember to do the things that please him. Maybe it's only the dry cleaning, the holes in the socks, the letters to be mailed, or the milk to be brought from the store. But forgetting them creates tension.

Fights are also provoked with "I told you so." The words don't even have to be used, and they don't have to be said in exactly that fashion. But there is nothing more likely to put someone down than to have a knowing smile on your face when some decision of his turns out badly.

Furthermore, I can treat my spouse in a condescending way. It may not be maliciously intended, but it comes across as if I'm treating him like a little child. I'm taking care of him all the time, protecting him against his mistakes or from other people taking advantage of him. Oh, a superior attitude is an excellent way to push the other person's temperature up to the boiling point.

Do you always fight about the same things?   *Your answer:*

In most marriages, fights tend to fall into patterns. We fight about the same things again and again. The things themselves are not necessarily big or terribly important. They may be little, like the time of meals or a certain TV show or where we're going to spend an evening. Or they may be bigger, like a relationship with in-laws or who our friends are going to be. We can learn a lot if we isolate those topics. Then we can look behind them and see what causes misunderstanding. Maybe we can discover some of the facets of our own personalities and of our relationship with each other that are really causing the fights. For it's not the topic itself that causes the fight. It's the lack of understanding and appreciating each other.

It's not the *subject* that is touchy. It's *we* who are touchy about the subject. There is a big difference here. It's easy to kid ourselves and say it's understandable to get upset about your mother or about burned meals or an unbalanced checkbook. But not everybody gets upset about those things—even though they may happen more frequently in other people's marriages than they do in ours. But every marriage does have things that cause dissension between husband and wife. The dissension comes from the absence of appreciation for each other and an unwillingness to listen in the areas in which we are sensitive.

That is it. It's our sensitivity that causes the fight, not the mother-in-law. The topic is irrelevant in itself. It's not the unbalanced checkbook, it's that having it balance matters to me and since you don't balance it, I hear you saying you don't care about me. I have to take on the fuss and bother of straightening it out. If I meant anything to you, you'd do it right. Or, if you really loved me you'd love my mother; you'd understand why it's important for me to see her or to be on the phone with her.

We have to face into, not the topic, but the touchiness of the other person. I have to find out what you are saying beyond the position you're taking. I need to respond to your need for attention or understanding or healing. Too often we hammer away about the topic, trying to prove each other wrong. But it doesn't make any difference who is right or wrong. We're both wrong because we're driving a wedge that separates us. The topic lies there on the floor between us. Any time one of us picks it up, the other immediately puts the gloves on. That's wrong.

It is up to me to search for what is upsetting you in what I'm saying about your mother or doing with our checkbook. I should do it not in order to put you down, but to develop empathy and understanding and a tenderness toward you.

Husbands and wives can fight about the same thing for years and never solve the problem. But the problem is not the decision they're trying to make or the positions they're upholding; it's their lack of communication. They're not even interested in communicating. Each just wants his own way. They're interested in having the other person listen; they're not at all interested in doing any listening themselves. My problem is that in certain topics I'm out to win. I'm out to beat you down. I'm out to prove myself right. I'm ignoring you. Instead, I've got to focus on you—and us together.

What starts your fights?   *Your answer:*

It's easy to blame a fight on something the other person has done or said, or on something he has not done. I'm aware of your involvement in our fights—and unaware of my own. I look on my part in the fight as inevitable and minor. I'm defending myself, I'm reacting to an unreasonable request, I'm pushed beyond endurance. I accuse you of doing wrong and overlook my part in it. I consider my part as something that any reasonable person would do in the same circumstances.

Basically, what any fight comes down to is that each of us has a non-negotiable position on topics. We go into the conversation determined that it will turn out our way. But as long as we have non-negotiable positions, we can't even talk about the topic. We need to start by talking about our non-negotiability, the reasons for our unwillingness to change. We need to consider what is happening to our relationship and how we can open up. It doesn't mean I have to surrender my position; it doesn't mean I have to subjugate myself to the other person. But it does mean that if I am absolutely and irrevocably committed to my position, I'm not involved in a discussion at all, I'm involved in a proclamation. There is no way anybody can respond except by fighting back—or saluting.

Another element that triggers fights is a sense of loneliness or a feeling of not being appreciated. I may have little self-appreciation or awareness of self-worth. So I tend to look for a scapegoat. I want to blame you. I put unreasonable demands on you in order to make this feeling go away. I see you as being responsible for my

Hey, we love each other!
Let's touch 'n' talk.

interior longing or insecurity. I consider you insensitive because you haven't noticed that I'm there and that I'm suffering. Maybe I don't blame you for having caused my pain, but I tell myself that neither are you taking the pain away.

It comes down to this: almost all fights are started by selfishness—selfishness on both sides, either by deliberate insensitivity to the other person, or because of a self-centeredness that wants the other person to do something for us or to stop doing something to us. We're not thinking of each other; I'm just thinking about myself and what I'm getting out of this relationship. Fights are always I-centered; they're not we-centered. They start because *I* want something or *I* don't want to give you something you would like to have. Maybe *I'm* not satisfied or *I* want you to change. Many fights start because we try to get our husband or wife to become the kind of person we want them to be. The reason? We have our ideal of what a husband or wife should be, and see that the other person is not living up to it, so we start to push. We don't accept our beloved as he is.

Is one of you always the loser?

Your answer:

Just as in a lot of marriages one person is always starting or provoking the fights so, too, one person is almost always the loser—or at least comes out on the short end of any fight. It is tremendously frustrating to always be on the losing end. Maybe the winning spouse is a better fighter because of being able to articulate a position well. Maybe the wife just can't compete against her husband's logic, and whenever they get into a fight he just "out-logics" her. He zeroes in on the situation and lines up all sorts of reasons and arguments. She doesn't want all those reasons and arguments; she just wants his attention. In his "reasonableness" he's denying her that attention.

Or maybe one has a better memory. The "rememberer" can bring up all sorts of past events or circumstances to prove his point. So the spouse is on trial. He can't compete because he doesn't even remember the event, much less the circumstances surrounding it. He has no answers. So he gets detailed to death. He retreats from such a confrontation shaking his head, knowing he's going to lose because he doesn't have the skill the other person is using.

It is a bad situation in a marriage if both husband and wife know who is going to be the winner before they even start fighting! They go through the whole charade realizing that only one of them will be the sufferer. The one who knows ahead of time that he will win is above it all and out of it—in a teaching type of role. It's like a phony wrestling match—the winner is predetermined. There is no equality. The person who loses always feels less significant in the relationship. He knows that in the long run he's going to be "proved" wrong. It leads to despair. He either withdraws more and more and becomes a peace-at-any-price person, or he gets very nasty in order to hurt the other. He's trying to bring some kind of equality into the relationship.

Another unfortunate aspect of the constant winner is that he never has to face the issue that has been raised. All he's doing by his tactics is winning. Nothing beneficial to the couple's relationship is happening. When fighting is totally one-sided, there is something sadly missing in the awareness of each other. If one side is always right, the relationship is not a normal one.

Do you deliberately hurt each other?

Your answer:

Fighting is not necessarily the worst possible thing that can happen in a marital relationship. It's not good. There is wrong in it because there is pain involved. But that kind of hurt is sometimes preferable to the pain of isolation and loneliness that can come about through *lack* of fighting. Fighting may have better results than the distance between two people that leads to a cool, dispassionate way of living together.

However, one of our worst faults in a fight is our deliberate effort to hurt the other person. The old saying "You only hurt the one you love" is true because only the one you love lets you get close enough to know his special weak points, the ones where he is most sensitive. It is dirty pool to attack the other person's sensitive areas. In a way, it's like my deliberately grabbing a person's arm and squeezing it at a sore spot precisely because I know it is sore.

Why do we do it? Because we're undergoing pain and we're retaliating. There is a certain revenge motive. We're saying, "I want to hurt you because you're hurting me."

When we're fighting, we need to remember that we're still married. We still love each other. Even though right now you're not very attractive to me, I can't put down and destroy what I really want to treasure, and what I'm hoping to treasure again shortly.

When I put my wife down, I'm putting myself down. When I deliberately sting my husband, I'm putting venom into myself. I've made him less in the eyes of both of us; consequently it's going to be harder for him to be his full self with me afterward, even when we have made up.

All of us have a fundamental mean streak in us. Instinctively we lash out at the jugular vein of the other person's sensitivity. We have to face into the issue and discipline ourselves to not be personal. If we're fighting about who our friends should be, I don't have to attack your motive for choosing this friend over that one. I don't have to describe that friend's characteristics in negative terms or call him derogatory names.

Sometimes in fights we say things to each other we would never think of saying to any other person in the world. No one else would stand for it! We do it partly because of our security in each other. Our attitude is: "He/she has to put up with it because we're married." Actually, it's because we're married that we shouldn't have to put up with it. Why do we believe it's less bad to deliberately hurt our husband or wife than it is to hurt a friend? Actually, the opposite is true. It's easier for somebody who doesn't live with me to get over my tongue-lashing than it is for someone who is constantly in my presence.

It is devastatingly true that if we say these things often enough, our spouse will come to believe them. He will tend to become the way our lambasting has pictured him. We say he's a lazy bum; that she's a gossip. Sooner or later these statements become self-fulfilling prophecies.

What are the good things about your fights?

Your answer:

One of the best things about a fight is that it clears the air. We get the thing out that has been festering inside one or both of us and has been causing us to draw apart. It is a positive step to talk over and honestly face the things that have led to our misunderstanding. When we get the misunderstanding out of the way we're back to facing into each other. We stop thinking of what the other person is doing or not doing, or how we feel. Our relationship perks up. We get a fresh start, a changed environment, a new lease on life.

Joe is a very easy-going kind of guy. He has an even temper. That's one of the things his wife, Susie, finds most attractive about him, but sometimes it drives her up a wall. She doesn't know where she stands with him. There are times when she doesn't find out until weeks later that Joe has been upset.

One day Joe blew his top. "Susie, don't you ever run out of breath? I've been trying to tell you about my new assignment at work. I'm nervous about it and I've been wanting to talk it over with you. But you're nonstop! There's no way I can get a word in edgewise. It's yap, yap, yap. You never shut up. It's like being married to a record player."

Susie was stunned. She flared back, "So now you want to talk and I'm supposed to figure that out. What am I—a mind reader?"

They went back and forth in the heat of anger for a while and then they both relaxed a little. Joe's frustration was out in the open. Susie realized that in the future she would have to be careful to recognize that just because Joe wasn't saying anything, it didn't necessarily mean he had nothing to say!

Another good thing to come out of fighting is that we both recognize how we've been trying to get around each other *without* fighting. We've been trying to get our way without letting the other person know what is important to us. One is supposed to guess at what's important, or have some kind of magic capability to read the other's mind. A fight can help us learn, at least for a time, to be more open, to get things out before they build up into a big hairy problem.

The reconciliation after a fight also brings a plus into marriage. It brings healing and a heightened awareness of each other. Couples laugh about "the best part of a fight being the making up." There is truth in that. We become more conscious of how important we are to each other. That is a precious value! We even become aware of how stupid we've been to have had to fight. If we would have talked the situation out in the early stages, we wouldn't have had to fight about it.

What are the bad things about your fights?   *Your answer:*

Not ending a fight is probably the worst thing about most fighting. To seek an armistice but not to have real peace is terrible. There is only an absence of war for a certain period of time. When a couple are exhausted or frustrated and stop hostilities only long enough to re-arm and get more ammunition to fire at one another, they're in bad shape. Fights should be fought through to the end. If they're left unsettled, both of us realize (at least instinctively) that they're going to happen again and again and again. It might be over a certain topic or an aspect of our relationship. We know that every time it comes up we're going to have the same difficulty with each other, and that war will keep erupting on this front. We need to stay with the fight, settle it and find each other. That is what a fight has to be about—to find each other.

The reason we don't, or can't, settle it is that both of us are unwilling to change our positions. We insist on unconditional surrender by the other person. Of course, the longer it goes on the more entrenched we get in our positions.

There are many ways to avoid finishing a fight. It can be by mutual agreement. Both of us throw up our hands in disgust and say, "What can we do! There is no solution." We drop it and never want to face the issue again. We have no confidence that there is ever going to be any kind of amicable settlement. We resolve never to be trapped into this kind of situation again and swear to go our own way on this. But despite all our intentions, the thing surfaces repeatedly.

Another way to avoid finishing a fight is for me to dissolve into tears. It isn't that I can't or shouldn't cry during a fight—that is perfectly legitimate—but I shouldn't become a puddle. There is no way you can fight with a puddle.

Still another way is for me to go storming out of the house or to walk off in solitary dignity into my bedroom and sulk. Or, I can create such a threatening atmosphere that you are terrorized into silence, afraid of what I'll do or what my anger is going to do to you. We are both apt to fall into a hostile quiet in which we walk around each other for a period of time until we decide to talk again.

Having an unending war is being married to a position rather than a *person.*

Holding grudges is also a devastating mistake in fighting. It's terribly debilitating when both husband and wife are prone to do so. However, in the case of Andy and Jean, only Andy had difficulty forgiving and forgetting. It took him days to get over a fight. After an incident in which Jean told him he was immature about money, Andy kept nursing his wounds, remembering the hurtful words Jean had said. Of course, he was not conscious of his own spiteful words, but he thought they were justified under the circumstances.

Obviously, this was an instance of self-centeredness. Andy was blotting out Jean's tenderness and sensitivity toward him. He was concentrating on what was done to *him,* how badly *he'd* been treated and how misunderstood *he* was. He built it all up in his own mind. He was trying to convince himself that he was right. In effect, he was talking to himself rather than to Jean. It was a form of inflicting punishment on her. He was implicitly saying to her that it was going to take one day or two days or five days to make up with him for what he considered abuse or injustice.

Then Andy met his friend Jack for lunch and started to tell him about Jean. Jack finally broke in on the tale of woe and said, "Look, Andy, why don't you grow up? Jean must be a saint to live with you. You carry on a fight forever. That's just nasty. Don't tell me you can't help it—that's nonsense. You nurse those grudges. Make up your mind to give Jean a break and start thinking about her good points and telling her about them instead of going over and over again in your mind how badly you're treated."

Andy wouldn't give Jack the satisfaction of knowing he had gotten through, but that night when he came home he deliberately tried to be cheerful and to praise Jean for the nice dinner and the loving way she dealt with the kids. The evening was a happy one and Andy felt free of a burden. He was actually relieved that he had called a stop to his brooding.

The best fights are sharp, swift and over with, so that we can be on our way again. We can look on such a fight as a momentary distraction. We got off the track but now we're back on it again. We're together and we're rolling again—as a couple. Grudge-keeping is a cancer in a relationship. In a way, it's a form of blackmail. I extort from you a certain plea for forgiveness. Until I see enough obvious distress or get what I consider a high enough level of pleading, I hold onto my grudge.

There is a temptation to excuse myself on the basis that this is the way I'm built—I can't help myself, and it takes me a long time to get over a fight. That's not good enough. I need to change. I have to discipline myself to change. Grudge-keeping is not good for me, it's not good for you and it's not good for our relationship. I have to learn to deal with my defect, to overcome it. Holding a grudge lengthens something that might be a one- or two-hour source of pain to days, weeks and sometimes even months. I can't tolerate a fault like that in myself. I have to take drastic steps to overcome this disease of mine.

Keeping score is also a bad aspect of fighting. It's almost like the old billiard room where there was a wire with knobs to keep score. Sometimes in a marriage both parties keep score just as accurately on how they're doing with each other. However, it doesn't matter who's winning or losing. In that type of situation, both are losers.

A fight has redeeming features—when it is faced on its own terms *right now,* in the present. What happened in the past, who won the last one and how many times I got my way in other fights, has nothing to do with it. To pull in the past is another way of carrying grudges. I'm not fighting just this fight, I'm fighting the last five. We have to take this moment by itself and not refer back to previous experiences. Then we have a chance.

Do you know what you're fighting about?   *Your answer:*

In a marital relationship, what often starts the fight is not the issue at all. Some little thing annoys me and it seems to be a good opportunity to put you on the defensive and nail you, so I blow up. Actually, something much deeper is eating at me. That is the cause of the fight. I use the little annoyances as a trigger to start something. I haven't been able to get anywhere on the main issue, so I keep picking at you on small issues that are only vaguely, if at all, connected with it. I get at the core issue indirectly because I don't want to face what's really bothering me.

Maybe I complain about your conduct when we were visiting a friend of mine last week. However, my real concern is your not liking my friend. That is the issue we have to face. Many times when I start a fight, I don't realize what is behind the specific thing I bring up. When we're going at it with each other we need to ask some personal questions. "What is really in my craw, what is bugging me?" "What is in your craw, what is bugging you?" Let's get what's really the matter out on the table instead of fighting about extraneous things.

It would be a tragedy if a husband and wife went through a fight and never unearthed the point of it or even realized they hadn't. A reason for numerous fights is that *couples don't know what they're fighting about.* They fight all around an issue and don't get to it. Because it's never settled, the problem comes up again in some other guise.

Kevin and Maureen repeated one of their fights recently. The evening started with periods of silence. Then each of them made remarks that could be taken either way. Then Kevin went too far with, "Whenever you're like this it's because you just spent a lot of money and you know I'm going to find out." Maureen flared back with reference to the fact that the Scotch were Celts, too. The air filled with accusations of spendthriftiness, irresponsibility, cheapness, pettiness. They had been through all this many times. It was like seeing a rerun of a bad movie.

Finally Maureen had to go to the bathroom. In that brief interlude she saw that the attacks weren't getting them anyplace. When she rejoined Kevin she said, "Let's start again. I said a lot of things I didn't mean and I'm sorry. You worry about money a lot. Why? What's behind it?"

Kevin was thunderstruck. With a great deal of effort he began to unload. "I guess it's because we never seem to be able to get ahead at all. Every time I get a raise you look on it as that much more to spend. I see myself as just a money machine. I bring the paycheck home every week—and that's what I'm supposed to do. I don't spend anything on myself—and that's OK, but I get regular raises and you're pleased for only a couple of days and then it's old hat. I'm just taken for granted around here. Whatever I accomplish is what you think I should be doing, so there's nothing special about it. I guess when I complain about money I'm doing the same thing you do when you say no to sex. I'm saying, 'Pay attention to me. Don't take me for granted! I have feelings, too.'"

Maureen wanted to defend herself but she knew that wasn't the point. This was a real change. Kevin was being open and she could stop him by being defensive or she could listen to him and his needs. She realized she hadn't been thinking about the pressure on him and had assumed that he knew how much she appreciated all he did for her. But she winced as she thought about how seldom she had told him.

"Kevin, how can I help?" said Maureen.

"Recognize that you're not independently wealthy and that I'm important to you and the kids. I need to hear that from you."

The real problem was out in the open. Now they could deal with it and make progress.

Do you use third parties in a fight?

Your answer:

There are obvious ways of using third parties to try to get you to come around to my way of thinking. I describe what my dad thinks of you, or what the guys I work with think about wives who act the way you do, or what the women in the neighborhood say about husbands who do "that." But those are obviously crude ways of using third parties.

We often use third parties much more subtly. I take the advice of other people and "stand up for my rights" and "won't let you lead me around by the nose." The other people can be friends or the author of an article on marriage. I approach our relationship determined to mold you into the way the books say you should be. Or because of a psychology book about marriage, I'm determined to "win my freedom" or "get my independence" or "maintain my dignity." Instead of facing into you I let somebody else's ideas or norm or judgment determine our relationship. In that situation, you are fighting an army. I'm buttressed by all sorts of "authorities" on what to say or positions to take or ways to conduct myself in order to get what I want. There are all sorts of shadow figures when we're fighting. I have my mind set. It's going to come out my way.

Part of the reason for my closed mind is that I have to make a report to the other women or to the other guys, and I don't want to come back to them the loser. The result of the fight should be determined by the two of us and what happens in our relationship without worrying about other people evaluating the result of our fight. When a wife knows she's going to have to talk to her girlfriends about the fight, or at least listen to them talk about their fights and how they came out, she holds out much longer and is much stronger in a fight and much more determined to win. The husband gets into a fight determined that it come out a certain way because of what fellow workers or buddies on the golf course have told him. Even though a man or woman may not talk about the fight to their friends, they have in their minds what those friends would think about them if they were to lose the point.

What type of fights do you have?

Your answer:

Maybe we can't get through to the other person so he has resorted to fighting to get us to listen. Maybe if we give him a little more care and attention and were more sensitive, the frequency and intensity of our fights could be sharply reduced. Maybe we're callous and don't notice the other person until he hits the ceiling. It may be hard for us to admit—or even see—that we don't pay enough attention; this is something we might well talk over with each other. Why do we fight? It may come out that the fights are largely caused by a pattern of not listening. Listening is a great preventive medicine for fights.

The length of fights can say something about our relationship. Sometimes we carry on fights forever. They may not be the shouting kind of fights. We may practice a quiet coolness or even a devastating politeness. We let the other person know that he hasn't won his way back into our favor. In that kind of cold war, we've decided to live together but not to be with each other and for each other.

It's a big mistake to keep silent—to avoid communicating. Actually, through their silence, a couple is really screaming at one

A special treat to celebrate our deeper love.

another! Their body language, their non-verbal talk, makes it quite clear where they stand. The problem is not a lack of communication. It's the kind of communication and the message being sent that is mattering a great deal.

Are you able to see the other side in your fights?

Your answer:

In a fight we're self-centered—I'm concerned about what is going on inside *me,* what *my* position is. My getting across *my* position, how you are treating *me,* are you listening to what *I* say? I don't look at how I'm coming across to you, what I look like to you, and whether my listening is acute or not.

It might be a good thing for a husband and wife in the middle of a fight to stop and take a five-minute breather. They need not regroup their forces or get more ammunition to hurl, they can look at themselves and see just what they're doing, how they're coming across, their tone of voice, their motivation, their attitude toward their partner at this moment. They can stand before a mirror and repeat their last couple of statements in the same tone of voice, with the same facial expression as they've just used. It will then be easier for each of them to understand why the other person is so turned off and so upset!

Also, we can ask ourselves, "If I saw things from the other's point of view, would I think it was important to do such-and-such a thing?" If we can get outside of ourselves a little bit and see from the other person's side, it might help us to be more reasonable, more understanding, warmer and more tender.

It will also help us to put things in perspective. When we get into a fight because we've been hurt, we respond to our feelings and are out to get the other person. We don't pay attention to his goodness or worth. We just see how he's hurt us, his mistakes, his bad qualities. We need to step back and look at ourselves to see what we're doing to cause trouble and how *we* can change.

Among the greatest mistakes we can make in any human relationship, but most especially in marriage, is to try to change the other person. That causes fights galore and intensifies them once we get into them. So we've got to make a resolution not to try to change each other, and to recognize what we're doing when we try. A big help in that recognition is this pause to look at ourselves.

How do you make up?   *Your answer:*

Every couple have their own specific style—or signals—to indicate that the storm is passing and they want to get together again. It might be a slowing down of the pattern of speech or a softening of the voice. It might be a relaxing of muscles, especially of the face. It could be an open admission that the other person has a point. It could be a reaching out of the hand and an appeal to enjoy each other rather than to keep beating each other over the head. It might be an honest and sincere "I'm sorry."

The particular way we make up is not important. But it's vital for both husband and wife to come to the decision to make up. Fights never end accidentally, nor do they end because one side has won by totally persuading the other. Fights are finished only when both husband and wife make the decision to face into each other once again and forget about the issue.

This decision is never easy, whether we make it near the beginning of a fight or after an extended period of battling. There is no magic formula that makes me want to stop fighting. There is no word you can say to change my mind. I have to honestly and sincerely come to grips with myself and decide whether I want to win my point or love and be loved. That is the fundamental question. We get into fights because we want to get something or to stop something. We'll decide to make up only when we realize that it's far more important for us to be in communion with each other than it is for us to get our own way.

Fights don't just fade away, either. We have to choose each

No matter what's happened, let's be together.

other rather than our positions. The difficulty is our *pride*—we constantly resist what we see as surrender, as giving up. We have to find where we are and decide whether or not we want to stay there. Our temptation, of course, is to say, "I'll give in when he gives in," or, "I'll be nice when she's nice." We can't do it that way. Neither of us has control over the other person; we can't make decisions for our spouse, and we can't excuse ourselves because of the activities of the other. I am responsible only for myself and my decisions. I have to decide, regardless of what the other person's response is, whether or not I want to make up.

We may have built up the pattern that one of us is the peacemaker—the one who says "I'm sorry" all the time—with the other accepting the peacemaker's apology or his seeking of forgiveness. One of us is always under pressure to make the first move. That is not right in a husband-and-wife relationship. It's never just one party who is the greater sinner, who is always wrong. I may be excusing myself on the basis that you can say "I'm sorry" more easily than I can. But it's not that I *can't* say it; it's that I *won't* say it. I may have to force it out. Maybe I have to write it out because I won't push the words beyond my teeth. But somehow I've got to do it.

Sometimes neither the husband nor the wife says "I'm sorry"— they stop attacking and just get together again. But this is not satisfying. It ignores the damage that has been done to the relationship. It prevents their restoring each other.

Because an issue and a fight have highlighted our differences and expanded the distance between us, it isn't enough to settle only the argument. We have to settle *us*. We have to bring *us* back into focus and heal the wounds we've inflicted. A muttered "I'm sorry" is not good enough. We have to spend some time on highlighting *us*. In the making-up process, if I concentrate on how generous I am in forgiving or in letting things pass, I am still distracted from our coupleness, and we are apart from each other. I may still be harboring some resentments and in the back of my mind thinking that I'm going to say such-and-such the next time. Maybe the reason for breaking off the fight is that I've decided I've had enough. It's more painful for me to continue the fight than to give up or to restore the relationship. I'm not considering what I've done to you or how you are feeling.

I must not only make you clearly present to me, but also make sure that you know and experience how much I care, the empathy I have in my heart, the compassion I feel.

At the end of any fight, there has to be a decision by *both* to get back into relationship. There is a decision to *offer* the apology and a decision to *accept* it.

If we break off the hostilities and get back together again only to a certain extent, if I expect that you will break the truce or start the battle up again or go back to the same old way that started the fight in the first place; if I'm not very trusting in the beginning stages of our renewed relationship, then I'm still concentrating on myself—where *I* am and how *I* feel. There won't be a true healing until we're each concentrating on the other, being more aware of each other's pain than we are of our own.

In restoring each other, we have to express our ambition to be one again in terms that the other person can experience, not just in ways satisfying to ourselves. Pleasing myself in the way I say I'm sorry isn't good enough. What I say and do has to be meaningful to you—something you appreciate. I can't just say, "Well, I tried. I said the right words." Maybe you need to feel the warmth of my hand on yours. I can't say, "I stopped being angry and I stopped saying nasty things, so you should have known I was ready to make up." That's asking you to read my mind. Actually the attempt to make up has to be as explicit and insistent as the negative things we have been saying for the last half hour or the last three days!

Because one of the reasons for a fight in the first place is usually our conviction that the other person wasn't listening to us, wasn't hearing what was going on inside us, we should be equally concerned with our spouse's listening to us when we want to be reconciled. Do we give him/her a chance to listen to the tender things we are saying? Or do we just mumble them quickly and expect to be heard? It's funny that during the fight we are so insistent on getting our points across, so adamant about making the other person understand our position! But afterwards we tend to get tongue-tied and shy. We're not nearly so clear about our apology as we were about our attack.

An apology has to be clearly given—and honestly meant. It can't be given just because it's expected. It has to come from our hearts. When we mean it and do all we can to follow through, we're whole again.

How can you avoid fights?   *Your answer:*

One of the best ways to avoid fights is not to store things up. When I first recognize there is a misunderstanding between us or a coolness developing, I have to sit down with you and talk things out. Oftentimes I don't, not out of any bad motives but out of good motives. I don't want to bother you, or I think if I settle it for myself there will be less hurt involved. Or I figure that after all, I'm a big boy or girl now and I should be able to take these things in stride. I'm kind of embarrassed at my being so upset.

Unless I'm honestly and sincerely willing to be open and let you in to know what is going on inside me, I can't expect you to have any kind of sensitivity toward me. And it's much easier to talk about something in its beginning stages than after it's grown all out of proportion. Furthermore, sooner or later these things will come out. Yes, they can be bypassed for a time, but they're going to build up inside us, just waiting for the explosion. It's much better to have the problem aired early, helped along by gentleness and understanding without the heat of anger.

Because from our past history we know which areas are at the basis of most of our disagreements and disagreeableness, we should find out where we lack understanding. We don't talk it over in order to change each other's minds or to surrender our positions. We talk it over so that we can gain a greater depth of empathy for each other and for what we hold dear. If we take each touchy subject and explore it together, look behind it into each other to see the values we are protecting, we can come closer together and prevent the areas of disagreement from creating a larger and larger distance between us.

If instead of trying to solve something, we try to learn what is going on behind the position—what is important to the other person—we will understand each other better. The goal is not to try to change each other but to get a greater comprehension and awareness of what each of us is really like. This is a form of preventive medicine. We want to prevent the kind of pain and hurt that we've inflicted upon each other in the past.

There is another way to avoid fights, or at least to make them less frequent. When we recognize we're out of sorts with each other, we need to physically touch. It's very difficult to stay apart from you when we're touching. It's difficult to concentrate on the distance between us when I'm holding your hand or feeling your face.

Touching makes us aware of each other in a special way. What commits us to a fight is our blotting out our awareness of each other. If we concentrate on increasing our awareness, we will have fewer fights. And when we do have one, it won't be so divisive. Our hands have a magic in them when it comes to fighting. It's hard to deliver even a verbal punch when we're holding hands.

Just as we can hurt each other, we can heal each other.

HEALING

Have you ever hurt your spouse?

Your answer:

According to the old saying, the saddest words of tongue or pen are "might have been." But I feel the saddest ones are "You only hurt the one you love." It's only people who are close and dear to us who can hurt us. It's our family and, most especially, our own husband or wife who inflict the deepest pain. They know our weaknesses, our vulnerable points. Unfortunately, in a disagreement, people who love each other tend to attack those weak points.

More than anybody else, people who love each other hurt each other. We're in frequent and close contact, with many opportunities to rub against each other and cause friction. Moreover, we have high expectations of the other person. We constantly look for him to provide all sorts of satisfactions. We expect him to understand us better than anyone else. We don't always look to other people to provide us with personal satisfaction, but we do expect it from our husband or wife.

In a husband-and-wife relationship, we're also likely to pick at each other. I try to get you to back down and give in. Interestingly enough, we don't do that often with other people; we're more understanding of them, more willing to protect their ego; we're careful not to back them into corners, causing them to make rash decisions. We exhibit much more respect for them as persons, protecting their dignity more than we do that of our husband or wife.

If we look back on our relationship with each other we probably can see a distinct pattern of hurt—on both sides.

We're apart and hurting —
let's change that.

Most of the pain we inflict stems from selfishness. I look around and say, "Hey, what am I getting out of all this?" "You're not paying attention to me." "Don't I have any rights around here?" "I'm not being treated with any respect." "I can't let you walk all over me." "It's not fair for you to pull me around by the nose."

One of the clearest indications of an approaching hurt is my starting to think that I'm being treated unfairly. Actually, fairness is not central to a marriage relationship. Marriage should be based on a total giving on both sides! When I start thinking about how unfair you are to me, I'm looking on marriage as a business deal, a partnership, with a 50-50 arrangement rather than a full relationship in which I concentrate on what I can give rather than on what I can get.

I inflict hurt on you in order to pay you back or to get you to change some habit I don't like. I want you to provide some service for me. What I'm saying is that if you don't please me, I'll hurt you. I'll hurt you in proportion to the dissatisfaction I'm experiencing at the present moment. Just as sex or money can be used as a reward or punishment to get you to stay in line, so I can use pain or the absence of pain.

We justify the pain we inflict on our spouse by dismissing it with, "Well, that's the way marriage is," or, "After all, I've suffered hurts too." Or, "I'm human and I don't always do the right thing." We don't take seriously the hurts we inflict, but we're serious about the hurts inflicted upon us. We think our own hurt justifies the hurt we inflict. Furthermore, if we concentrate on our own hurt and pay little attention to what we've done to the other person, then their pain is not present to us. We're able to tolerate it very well.

Hurt in a marriage is a significant aspect of the husband-and-wife relationship. Couples need to learn how to deal with it—not to just get used to it or recognize that it's inevitable, but to face it. They need to look for the personal defects that lead them to inflict hurts or to be hurt when no harm was intended. They need to discover what they can do to lessen the hurt potential. This is one of the areas in which couple decisions should be made.

Ordinarily we wait until we are hurt before we try to cope with it. This is not a prudent way of handling things. Our track record indicates that we don't act our full selves when we're hurt. It would be far better if we learned from the past.

Often we hurt each other and don't even realize it at the time. That's understandable, but it's not excusable when it happens again and again over a period of years. We have to learn to discipline ourselves.

The wife of Pete, a close friend of mine, divulged to me how her recent birthday had been unusually wonderful. It seems that Pete was excited about doing something extra special for her.

He had chosen a card carefully and wanted her to know all that she meant to him. He had written:

> "Darling Jill, we've celebrated a lot of birthdays and I've written many loving words to you—which I've meant. But I've let you down more than a few times. I want this coming year to be different.
>
> "One thing I can't stand is to see any hurt in your eyes, especially when I bring it there. I know the way I talk about your mother pains you. I have to confess that sometimes I deliberately do it because I'm mad at you. I'm disgusted with myself.
>
> "So for your birthday present this year I give you my loving promise to speak nicely about your mother and to praise her qualities. This present is costing me more than any other I have ever given you, but I love you so much I am determined not to hurt you that way any more."
>
> All my love, Pete

Healing between husband and wife is a beautiful experience. It is very real and magnificent. However, it is a catch-up situation. The reason healing is necessary is that the hurt has been devastating. We can't excuse our hurting each other on the basis that healing is meaningful; we have to try to reduce the hurts. The human dimension is such that, despite our best efforts and greatest concern, we will still hurt each other because of our selfishness or carelessness. We really don't want to, do we?

After all, our whole ambition in life when we first met and got married was to bring joy and happiness to each other. Hurt is contrary to that ambition. So if we're sincere in saying that we love each other, we definitely have to make a commitment to work together to reduce the hurts, both in frequency and in depth. And we can't do it unless we talk everything out. We have to find out what hurts the other person. All too often, even after years of marriage, we don't know what his hurt points are; we don't take them seriously enough; we don't realize how much certain words or actions sting. Caring, we'll find out. When we know, we can take steps to avoid the hurt.

We can put into words the feelings we experience when we are hurt, so that our beloved gets a true understanding of what we're going through.

Then we can talk over our experiences of being healed. This is sure to involve each other's goodness in attempting to be careful—not primarily of topics, but of each other. Because of that carefulness, the hurt was either sharply reduced or wasn't experienced at all. Talking about this shows us what *good* habits we have and enables us to develop them even more.

Furthermore, we have to talk over where our carelessness lies and where our insensitivity is.

Together we can make a real commitment to attack hurt as a couple. We will make a tremendous all-out effort, using every means at our disposal, to conquer the cancer of hurt that we've experienced over the years. We'll do everything we can to build up the understanding and the openness we need to help us be so conscious of each other that we won't even get near to causing hurt.

How often do you heal each other?

Your answer:

If we heal each other frequently, it shows there's a lot of hurt between us. Healing is not something that is cheap or easy, nor is it always accomplished. It's a tremendously wonderful experience, but like physical healing in the sense of miracles, the healing of the spirit is not common; it is not an everyday happening.

In all probability the occasions of healing in our relationship are brilliant stars in our sky. It's good to reflect on them. Nothing is more refreshing, nothing can make me feel warmer toward you, than those moments when you put me together again, when you bring me back from the depths of hurt.

Healing has a tremendous immediate impact on us and we very much appreciate it, but sometimes we soon forget about it. When it passes again through my mind I may smile or feel very warm, but then go on to something else. Actually, the more I reflect upon the healing, continually making it alive to me, the more capable I will be of experiencing it again and of granting that experience to you.

If I don't recall any specific moment of healing in our relationship, I might think I have never hurt you very much. The excuse may indicate we aren't aware of each other's needs because we're calloused—or we try to heal ourselves. Both are bad experiences.

In the first case, we've developed callousness by keeping apart from each other. We have deliberately avoided letting the other person get through to us.

In the second case, we've also ignored our relationship. We don't want to put ourselves into the other's hands. I don't want to be dependent upon you for my healing. But it doesn't work. I can dispose myself to be healed, but I can't actually bring about the healing of myself by myself. I need to be in relationship with you.

Do you heal each other or do you do only a patch-up job?

Your answer:

Sometimes we try to let things blow over; we want to let bygones be bygones. We attempt to forget about a painful situation or at least to become less conscious of the hurt inflicted. That's a patch-up job. That's not healing.

In fact, we even talk about "patching things up" between us. It means we've come to an accommodation. We recognize that neither of us will give in, so each gives in a little or somehow makes do.

That's a charade. It's a make-believe sort of thing. We're just picking up the pieces and going ahead as if nothing had happened. But if we've hurt each other, something *has* happened. Claiming otherwise is deluding ourselves. Yes, a patch-up job is better than continuing the hurt, but we need to face into what has to be done.

Bev sometimes teased Tom in front of others about his relationship with his mother. He didn't like it at all and always got upset. Bev didn't do it often because it bothered him so much, but occasionally she couldn't resist the temptation. When she did, she usually apologized to him afterwards, figuring that made it all right.

One evening it suddenly came to her that Tom was genuinely deeply hurt when she teased him that way. She hadn't taken it all that seriously. "Tom," she said, "I'm upset with myself. I've been foolishly insensitive. I haven't cared about your feelings at all. I've been sorry because you were upset, but it never really bothered me. I see now how terribly I've treated you. I'm thoroughly ashamed. Please forgive me."

We have to heal each other, come to grips with each other as persons, blend again, become one. This goes far beyond just deciding not to stay mad any more, not to stay hurt, not to brood or withdraw. Healing calls for reconciliation. A couple needs to be aware of each other again; each has to be more aware of the other's hurt than of his own. They have to want to remove that hurt, not just skip over it. Each has to make sure the other person is whole again.

Are you constantly making up in the same areas?

Your answer:

Once a true healing takes place, it lasts. It's not something temporary. A constant repetition in the same area indicates something is wrong. We need to sit down and talk over why this is happening, but not just as a topic for discussion—it must be much deeper.

We have to ask ourselves, "Why does this upset one or the other of us so much?" "What is the circumstance, the statement, the action, that causes this type of hurt?" We need to ask each other, "Do you know what you're doing to me when you say or do things like that?" "How are the two of us going to work together so that this hurt doesn't continually recur?"

We can't just go over the same situation and keep making up all the time. It's much too painful that way. And it doesn't make any sense. We must take steps to see that it doesn't happen any more. We might say to ourselves that we can't help it, but we *can* if we really want to. One of the reasons we keep going over the same ground is that we haven't honestly seen the basics of the situation.

We excuse ourselves on the grounds that these things just happen. They *don't* "just happen"—and when they occur consistently, there's something in us we have to change so that they don't "happen" any more.

What is the difference between "forgive me" and "I'm sorry"?

Your answer:

Both phrases seem obvious and simple. We use them interchangeably, saying, "Please, won't you forgive me?" or, "I'm sorry for what I've done." But the two words "forgive" and "sorry" express two completely different experiences. However, since we've reduced both words to the meaning of "I'm sorry," we've eliminated a great richness and meaningfulness from our life together.

"I'm sorry" means I recognize that what I did was not right. It was not right for me as a husband or as a wife to act the way I did. I want to take back what I've done. I want to wipe away what I've said. The right thing for me to do in the circumstance is to apologize to you. When I'm sorry I generally try to find some excusing circumstance—maybe that I was tired or upset, careless and not thinking. I should have known that you were having a bad day. I should have remembered that you're sensitive about this. I don't want you to take so seriously what I've done.

I may well be ashamed of myself. I may see what I've done as something not worthy of me and not what you should expect from me.

When I say, "I'm sorry," I want you to tell me that everything is OK between us. I want you to tell me to forget what I've done—it's all over—it's all right; now that I recognize I've been wrong, it's over with.

Forgiveness is something entirely different. In "I'm sorry" it's *I* who am sorry. In "forgive me" the emphasis is on *you*. When I seek forgiveness, I'm focusing on our relationship. I see that our relationship is not right because of me. What I've done has determined where I am with you. My insensitivity toward you, my unawareness of you, is a breach of our relationship. I'm not concentrating so much on what I've done as on where I stand with you. The forgiveness is centered around my hurting our relationship rather than on what I've done or not done or the words I've said or not said.

In asking forgiveness, I don't try to excuse myself. It's not that I did a wrong thing and I'm looking for you to excuse me. Instead I know *I'm* wrong, not only in what I did, but because I put myself, my comfort, my interests—or whatever—before "*us*." I recognize that there's something between us that has to be cleared up and, more than that, *I'm* what's between us. It isn't that what I've done isn't worthy of me; it's that *I'm* not worthy of *you*. So I place myself in your hands. I put myself at your mercy. In a sense I propose to you all over again, asking you to accept me as your husband or wife.

Obviously, forgiveness is not over some piddling little situation in which an individual forgets to pick up the milk or darn the socks. Forgiveness is necessary with a violation of relationship, such as Ben's being more involved in his job than in Madeline, his wife. Or Madeline's being totally committed to the kids and not listening to Ben. Or Ben's keeping to himself and not letting Madeline inside him to know the real Ben. These are very real breaches of relationship. They call for a seeking of forgiveness rather than just an "I'm sorry." Maybe Ben realizes that the loneliness Madeline is experiencing is the result of his not spending enough time with her. Or Madeline realizes that her lack of appreciation is causing the quiet desperation Ben has—as he pours out his life in a meaningless or thankless job to support her.

This type of discovery and self-revelation can't be responded to simply by a resolution that he or she will do better—that Ben will pay more attention to Madeline, that Madeline will say thank you to Ben more frequently, or that Ben will listen a little bit better or spend more time with Madeline. They have to realize that this thing has caused a breach between them. They are experiencing a separation in spirit, whether it has existed for a day or a week or for years. Actually, they don't gain awareness of the situation through self-examination. They gain it through seeing the goodness of each other. Ben realizes how he is not living up to Madeline. Madeline realizes how she is not living up to Ben. An apology is self-centered and not apt to produce insight. Forgiveness is totally other-centered and very likely to give deep insight.

The Prodigal Son's turnabout did not happen just because he looked at what he had done; it happened in terms of his father. He saw how wonderful his father was. He did not go back to his father and say, "OK, I've learned my lesson, I'm going to stop all the bad things I've been doing." No, he went back to his father and stated very honestly and humbly that he had failed as a son, let his father down, betrayed his father's goodness. That was where his unworthiness lay. His sin lay not so much in *where* he went (to evil and licentious living) as *from whom* he went. Forgiveness centers not on what I have done, but on whom I *haven't been* to you!

Seeking forgiveness isn't very natural to us. We don't do it casually or easily. I have to have your help. It is something a couple works on together. It's not an individual talent or blessing that a husband or wife has. It is something we develop in each other. Husbands and wives should talk over how to build up a desire to want forgiveness and how to ask for it. Yes, it's difficult to even want forgiveness. It's easier for me to say, "I'm sorry" or "Well, yes, I did a bad thing." To focus in on you and your goodness, seeing myself in those terms, takes a lot of manhood or womanhood. In order to develop that in our relationship, we have to do it together.

One night Dick said everything he could to hurt Sherry. She was bewildered and anguished.

He was concerned all the next day. What was Sherry going to say when he got home? More important, what was he going to say? This wasn't something he could pretend hadn't happened. He knew he couldn't just walk in and be especially nice. He was going to have to face into himself and Sherry.

When Dick walked through the door he saw that Sherry's eyes were red and puffy. She stiffened as he went to hold her and she turned away. Dick held on to her and gently turned her face so that he could look into her eyes. "Honey, last night I was ugly. Saying I'm sorry just doesn't cover that. I want you to forgive me. I need your forgiveness to make me whole again."

The film disappeared from Sherry's eyes, her muscles gradually unwound as she leaned against him and held him tight. Tears of relief welled up in her eyes and after a few moments she whispered, "I forgive you."

Later Sherry said, "Thanks for doing that. I was all set for a stormy session. I was going to make you see how horribly you had treated me. When you asked me to forgive you my heart stopped. I quit thinking about how bad you were and began to realize I wasn't perfect either. Who was I to grant forgiveness? You were sincere and put yourself in my hands. I will never forget it. I believe forgiveness has to be the greatest moment of closeness two human beings can ever have!"

Part of the difficulty is that the other person has been hurt and the natural instinct is to strike back or to hold back and get some kind of pledge that this is not going to happen again.

Too, it's hard for the other person to be approached and asked to forgive. Most of us would prefer to be asked to accept an apology. That's a lot easier to act on.

And, at the same time, when we want forgiveness the asking for it is hard. It is a humbling thing. We have to talk over how to go about it, how to express in sincerity and humility our desire to be forgiven.

If we become familiar with each other's minds and hearts, there's a much greater possibility that we will seek and grant forgiveness.

What is the difference between "I forgive you," "It's OK" and "Forget about it"?

Your answer:

When you seek my forgiveness I have to focus in on you—and us. I can't just look at what has been done to me, no matter how severe the hurt may have been. If I answer, "Forget about it," I mean for you not to pay attention to the thing you've done; it's all over with. I don't pay attention to it any more myself, and we can start again as if it had never happened. If I answer, "It's OK," I mean that it didn't really bother me, or I understood that you were having a bad day; or maybe it did get to me, but now I'm over it, so we can forget about it.

If I say, "It's OK," or, "Forget about it," to you when you have asked me to forgive you and you mean it, I have put you down. I'm refusing to accept your recognition of yourself and your desire to have our relationship fully reinstated. I concentrate on the thing instead of the person. I'm saying that I don't want you to be that close to me—that forgiveness is too intimate, so I'll treat your words as an apology.

When I say to you, "Please forgive me," I'm not primarily referring to what I have done; I'm saying that I haven't been part of you. I haven't lived up to you or to us. I haven't had you in the forefront of my consciousness. I haven't been living our relationship to the hilt. I've been bearing the name of husband or wife falsely (because I cannot be "wife" or "husband" without you). I want you to accept me home. I want to be back to "us" again. So

Forgive me for hurting you.

I'm asking your forgiveness because for a while I haven't really been yours!

The response to that petition has to be given on similar terms. You tell me that I'm forgiven, meaning that I'm whole with you again, that I'm yours and you're mine, that we belong to each other, fully and irrevocably. It's far deeper than "It's OK now," in which we're starting where we left off.

Seeking forgiveness and granting forgiveness puts us way ahead of where we were when the relationship was breached. Seeking forgiveness is an extraordinary gift to a beloved, and granting forgiveness is a gracious blessing to a spouse, so we're not where we were, we're more marvelously involved with each other than ever before.

When we say the words, "I forgive you," they cannot be

conditional or qualified, they have to be absolute. They mean we're together again, whole. You're absolutely my husband without any qualifications; you're absolutely my wife. The father of the Prodigal Son didn't look at what his son had done; he didn't compare him with the other son; he just saw his returned boy. A person who forgives has only to see his spouse. There's no attempt to forgive the deed itself. There's no attempt to excuse or exonerate the husband or wife. We're much beyond that when we're talking about forgiveness.

Seeking forgiveness and granting forgiveness are redeeming qualities in human beings. They have power to overcome pride and selfishness. The only way we can live up to this power is by being with each other, talking together, bringing out of each other the capability to ask or grant forgiveness. Often we don't even recognize we have the capability. We have to experiment, find out what we can do to put across our sincere desire for forgiveness or our genuine granting of forgiveness. Many times we don't know how to approach each other, so we can begin now by talking it over. I ask what is meaningful to you, and you ask me. I want you to know how I respond to you. I want you to experience the forgiveness in my heart.

When you forgive, do you remember the hurt or the reconciliation?

Your answer:

The person who is seeking forgiveness recognizes the hurt he has caused his beloved. He knows that the hurt is the reason he is seeking forgiveness. He's saying, "I know that a tremendous loneliness (or anger or insecurity or fearfulness) is going on inside you because of my failure to be present to you, to take you into consideration and to live my life with you in mind." I ask you to take your eyes off the hurt and focus on our relationship, and to say, "*We* are more important than the hurt."

When I am seeking forgiveness I am most aware, not of what I have done, but of what is going on inside you. If I look at what has been done to me, then I'm going to estimate it in terms of right and wrong and of how serious it is. But there's no need to even consider that, for when I say, "Please forgive me," I have already recognized the evil involved in my actions. I'm not defending myself at all, and though I'm certainly not bypassing what I have done, I'm focusing on something more important—what is going on inside you, the one who will be doing the forgiving.

Looking at the hurtful act misses the point; that's been handled, that's been taken care of, that has been recognized for what it was. The one who has been hurt is beyond it. He is at the point of forgiving the other person for breaking their relationship. He is concerned with the "we" of the marriage.

There's no implication that I shouldn't be feeling in need of forgiveness or that my reaction is exaggerated or unreasonable or oversensitive. When I seek forgiveness honestly and openly I place myself in your hands and ask, "Will you accept me as a sinner, or will you reject me?" "Will you accept my affirmation of your goodness, or will you insist upon your own way?"

You, the potential forgiver, have a basic choice to make. You can keep the hurt or you can take me back. Not me along with the hurt, but me alone, and in that way wipe out the hurt. If you maintain your right to keep your hurt, you are not fully accepting me. We are not reconciled.

When I say only, "I'm sorry," you have to ask yourself whether or not I really realize what I have done to you—if I have any idea of how much hurt I have inflicted on you. But when I say, "Forgive me," you never have to ask those questions, because those very words acknowledge that I am aware of the hurt within you. That's precisely why I am seeking forgiveness.

But you may not want to give up the hurt. The pain of being put down or ignored, or of not being appreciated or valued, is a sharp one. The loneliness of not being listened to or understood is real. Our hurt looms large on our horizon. We can become so engrossed in that hurt and in what caused the hurt that we fail to see the person of our beloved. We may hear the words seeking forgiveness, but not listen to them. As long as we keep our hurt to ourselves, we're married to our hurt and not to our husband or wife. When you ask my forgiveness because you have hurt me, the point is not that I am justified in being hurt, nor that it's perfectly understandable that I'm hurt. It is not important to ask, "How could you possibly have done this to me?" or, "What ever possessed you to be so insensitive to me?" Those questions are irrelevant right now. The only question that I have to face is whether or not I will forgive you.

I may be so upset and so absorbed in what's going on inside me that I don't want to face that question. A plea for forgiveness is asking me to deliberately and consciously turn away from myself and face out toward you, my beloved. Sometimes, of course, I say I will try to forgive you but that usually means I don't want to make a full-fledged effort. I want the pain to go away before I look at the question of forgiveness. But when the pain is gone, forgiveness is not needed! An apology or an acceptance of an apology may be needed, but forgiveness is not needed when the pain is gone.

Sometimes I forgive halfheartedly. I want to tell you that you are forgiven to make you feel better, because I really do love you and I want things to be back to normal with us. But I also want to keep looking at some of that pain. I want to keep some attention on what has happened to me—what I'm enduring. When I do that, I'm not trusting you. I'm saying I don't believe you are really seeking my forgiveness or caring about "us." I'm saying that if our relationship is renewed, if I place myself in your hands, I still won't get enough attention or sensitivity or understanding.

The Prodigal Son was afraid at first to go all the way in trusting. He didn't want to be restored to sonship. He didn't expect to be anything more than a servant in his father's house. But the father said that he wanted the boy to again be his son, with total trust on both sides. He wasn't content with taking care of his boy's needs, making sure he had enough to eat, clothing, and a roof over his head. No, the father wanted the relationship. The father was putting himself into the boy's hands, opening himself up to the possibility of being hurt again. He was affirming the relationship. That's what we must do when we're asked to forgive—we must affirm the relationship.

When you ask me to forgive you, my answer has to be much deeper than, "It's OK; I'll do the right thing by you, and we'll get along all right." We have to proclaim to each other that we belong to each other, that you are far more important to me than the hurt inside me. The hurt is nothing compared with you.

Sometimes, of course, because of our human weakness we say, "I forgive you," but we are still wary, still doubtful. We have not given the wholehearted, total yes that forgiveness calls us to. We need to ask our spouse for help. The very person who is asking forgiveness has to assist us in granting it. Just as he has placed himself in our hands, we have to place ourselves in his, so that he can help us fully grant forgiveness.

What are some of the barriers to forgiveness?

Your answer:

It's difficult to seek or grant forgiveness if we keep score. If we think our relationship has to be an even-Steven type of arrangement (we'll forgive only as often as the other person does) we have a mistaken notion of fairness—and forgiveness.

The moment of forgiveness is a total moment. It has nothing to do with the past or the future; it has to do only with the present. I'm not asking you to forgive me this time because I've forgiven you in the past. I'm asking you to forgive me because I need forgiveness at this moment. I recognize I have hurt you, and that's why I'm seeking forgiveness, not in order to even up the score.

The *granting* of forgiveness has to be on the same terms. It can't be in relationship to the past—that I forgive you because you forgave me last time or because you've asked me to forgive you many times before. It has to be a right-now thing; I have to forgive you *now*. It's a pure, self-contained moment. The event which caused the present turmoil or pain within me may have occurred some hours or days or weeks ago, but the forgiveness you are seeking now is for what I am going through at this moment. Not for what was done, but for what *is*. Not for a past event but for my personal experience of pain because of it.

Seeking forgiveness is calling for an act of faith. When I say, "Please forgive me," I'm saying, "Please believe me, because I know what pain you're experiencing. Believe that I care about you and that I want to heal that pain. Because of that hurt I am reaching out to you and trying to restore us to each other. Believe that I do recognize that I am responsible for where we are with each other." So when I say, "Will you forgive me?" the best response is, "Amen, I do believe."

Appearances can be terribly deceiving. The hurt may be more believable than the seeking of forgiveness. That is why we often fail to forgive. We say to ourselves, "But how many times do I have to forgive you for this?" When Jesus was asked how many times one is required to forgive, he answered, "Not seven times, but seventy times seven." That is the Jewish way of saying "constantly." So the only legitimate question is "Will I forgive you *this time*?" There is no other time. The past has already been accomplished. The future is an unknown that we shouldn't be concerned about. We're not asked to forgive the future, just this time. So the answer to the question, "How many times do I have to forgive you?" is "Once—*now*!"

**Do you demand change
before you will forgive?**
                              Your answer:

One of the signs of our faithlessness and our unwillingness to believe all that is involved in the other person's request for forgiveness is that we expect him to exhibit some real change before we will forgive. Actually, the real change is the change of heart he has already exhibited by seeking forgiveness. But we don't always trust that change. We at times imply that we'll forgive only if we see some evidence that the occasion for the hurt is not going to happen again. So in response to the request, we say something like, "We'll see," or, "Give me time," or, "How can I be sure it's not going to happen again?" There's no way the other person can guarantee his future sinlessness—that he's never going to fail us, that he will not let us down next Tuesday, or in the year 2000! Instead, we are concerned with where we are with each other right now. That's the only thing we have to face and respond to.

But we're so untrusting, so cautious, so fearful and conscious of our hurts, that we don't want to risk being hurt again. This is understandable, but we have to decide whether we want to close the door and be safe and secure in isolated loneliness or open up and have the possibilities of a deep relationship.

Our demand for a change of behavior as a guarantee of sincerity is not at all justifiable. It's not saying, "I trust you, I believe in you, I have faith in you." It's saying, "When your actions are acceptable to me, then I'll let you off the hook." It's like telling someone you trust him but want his terms in writing.

Naturally when you seek forgiveness you have to honestly and sincerely mean what you are saying, and that includes a deliberate, conscious attempt to avoid anything in the future that would hurt me. I must not look at whether or not you have failed in the past to carry out that intent. The question I ask myself is whether I believe you at this moment. Because of your past history in these circumstances, it may be hard for me to say Amen, but the difficulty of it is not the point. It's hard, but it's also simple. It's either a yes or a no. Not a maybe. Not "Let me think about it" or "Wait till I get over it."

Also, when I demand that you change, I put myself (the potential forgiver) in the role of judge. I stand over you and rule on whether you are worthy of being forgiven. I don't have any right to do that. That is arrogance of the first order. I am a sinner, too, and I've been forgiven much. It's like the Gospel story in which the king forgave a man his debts of huge amounts of money. Then that man went out and threw into prison a poor man who owed him just a few pence. I can't put myself in a position of judging you. When I do, it's I who need forgiveness.

When I act as judge I put you in a hopeless position. What possible response can there be? No matter how much good will or sincerity you may have in asking me for forgiveness, you know that I am already distrustful of you.

Moreover, we are apt to go back to that 50-50 doctrine—the insistence upon "fairness." We start to look outside of us to some objective norm. If I bring up that norm, you may even agree that it's fair for me to ask you to come through with some kind of guarantee because you have blown it so often in the past. But then our eyes are off each other and we're back on performance again. That's not what a marriage is all about.

Forgiveness involves not what has been done but how we are affecting each other. It's aimed at setting *us* straight, not at setting *things* straight. I might think that the worst thing that could happen would be for you to fail again and inflict future hurt on me. Wrong. The worst thing that could happen is for me to continue this present hurt by not granting you forgiveness. The hurt that *could come* is only a possibility, but the hurt that exists now is a *fact*. When you ask my forgiveness, you are asking me to live not with my hurt but with *you*. My hurt is not much of a companion, but *you* are, so this should be an offer I can't refuse.

**Are you willing
to forgive yourself?**   *Your answer:*

One of the greatest barriers in any relationship, but especially in the husband-and-wife relationship, is not just the difficulty of accepting the other person's forgiveness, but the difficulty of forgiving oneself. Sometimes it's easier to understand and forgive you, responding to you and your needs when you've hurt me, than it is to understand and forgive myself. Many times I just blame myself. I keep going over and over how bad I've been, what a mistake I've made, or how much pain I've inflicted. I don't see my own goodness.

As long as I don't forgive myself, I can't accept forgiveness. I don't see myself as forgivable. As in forgiving anyone else, forgiving myself is also a decision—I have to decide to do it.

What makes it hard to seek forgiveness or to grant it?

Your answer:

Probably the most difficult barrier to seeking or granting forgiveness is the devil of being "right." It's hard for us to forget about who is "right" and who is "wrong." If I'm the one granting forgiveness, it's tough to bypass my conviction that you were wrong. I don't want to forgive you because it means that I have to face into you. (It would be easier to face into the issue.) Forgiveness does not concern itself with who is right and who is wrong. It's strictly a case of my responding to you and saying, "I forgive you; we are whole again, we're back together again." But I often care more about hanging onto my being right, my position, than about getting in touch with you again.

It's even harder to give up being right if I'm the one asking forgiveness. I may view it as a confession that I was wrong, and I don't want to do that even though I may admit it to myself. I'd much rather forget the whole thing or shove it under the rug.

Isn't it tragic how the words stick in my throat when I have to say to you that I made a mistake? That I said something mean or unthinking? That I haven't been the person I promised you I would be when I married you? None of us want to come out with such an admission. We'd much rather have the incident blow over. I keep looking around for some excuse, something with which to defend my position. I want to tell you that I'm sorry you are hurt; I don't want to say I'm sorry because I was wrong.

Kathy prided herself on being a good wife. She worked hard at being compassionate, understanding and thoughtful of her husband, Paul. There were always little extra touches at meals. The

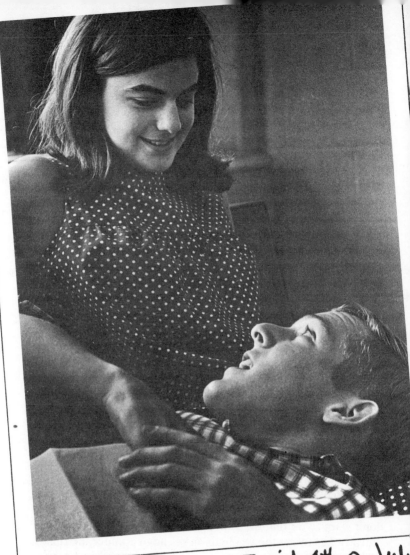

I remember being so stupid 4th of July
Thanks again for forgiving me

house was attractive and the children well taken care of. She agreed with *Love Story,* that love was never having cause to say you're sorry. There were times when she slipped, but in general, Paul didn't have much to complain about. She loved him and she was generous with her love. He always said so himself.

That's why she couldn't understand what happened one night. He hadn't been angry nor tried to hurt her. He'd said, "You know,

Kathy, you're one of those 90%-10% wives. You look on marriage as 90% your giving and 10% mine. You're great, but you've decided what a good wife is and what kind of wife I should have. It seems to me it's up to the man to decide what kind of wife is good for him. You're so busy living up to your model of a good wife that you don't have time to know me. The only purpose you've allowed me to have is to be someone you can do things for. I have no say in who you are to me at all."

She was confused, and Kathy didn't like to be confused. What did he expect of her? Suddenly it hit her. Paul wanted her to stop pleasing herself and look at him. All that she had supposedly been doing for him had been because it fitted into her view of a wife. Kathy wasn't used to being in the wrong. It was a very squirmish situation for her. She couldn't ignore what Paul had said. Just the thought of seeking his forgiveness made her stomach churn.

Again she realized she was thinking of herself and how she would look instead of what it would mean to Paul. Kathy decided if it was ever going to happen it better be right away. The more time she spent in thinking about it the more excuses she thought of.

That evening Kathy began: "Paul, I'm not very good at this because I've worked hard to avoid being in the wrong. I see now that I've created my own world and made you fit into it. Please, please forgive me. I want us to have a fresh start. I want to be *your wife* instead of my image of a wife." Paul held her tenderly, "We have a whole new world before us and this time it's *our* world. I love you!"

We can halt the pain for the other person and for ourselves by not stubbornly insisting on the justice of our cause, on the correctness of our judgment, on the justifiable nature of what we said or did. By dropping our self-defense, we discover what coupleness is all about—that we are to love each other and to be in close relationship. The only way that will happen is for us to seek and grant forgiveness.

Interestingly enough, we can read something like this in a book and recognize that it is stupid to let our pride, our stiff-necked attitudes, prevent us from growing in our relationship. Yet we find ourselves wanting to always be right even though it doesn't make any sense.

Other times when I'm seeking forgiveness, I want both of us to meet in the center of the field and each equally confess his error. Then it's a match, a toss-up. But then I'm not seeking forgiveness. I want you to say that you were wrong too and that both of us made mistakes.

One more point: when you seek forgiveness from me, I should not be cheap about it and make excuses for you. I need not start saying, "Well, I'm as great a sinner as you are." It's true and I may recognize that fact; I may even seek forgiveness myself, but right now you've asked me to grant you forgiveness. I must not distract from you and put the attention on me. I have to respond to you in the terms you ask. You have sought my forgiveness, so I must reach out and heal you.

Is one of you always the healer?   *Your answer:*

Hal couldn't ever remember saying that he was sorry to Marlene. He was sorry a lot of times and he showed it with flowers, a night out, and doing chores around the house that he had promised to get done but never had. But he never used the words. They stuck in his throat. Besides, he felt she understood.

Marlene always gave in when they had a fight. That's the way her mother had been and she figured it was the woman's role. Besides she couldn't stand the silence. And when she said, "Let's make up," Hal gave her extra attention and little favors.

One day she read that this type of situation was bad for both partners. That night she brought it up to Hal. "An article says that the one who's always making up says 'I'm sorry' but doesn't really mean it and carries a grudge. I find I do that with you. And I make sure you do plenty of things for me before I finally let it go. The more I think I'm right the more you have to do.

"The article also says that the one who never says he's sorry never really changes. He thinks he's right because the other person has given in or it's OK to act that way because he does all sorts of nice things afterwards. Don't you think that describes you, Hal? Why don't you ever say you're sorry? You say you can't but that's not true. It goes against your pride, but you can say the words. You just don't want to."

Hal shifted uncomfortably. He was uneasy with this conversation. But he did agree with Marlene. "Yes, if deep down I think I'm wrong I go all out to make it up to you, and you make sure I do. But why do I have to say the words? You know when I'm sorry."

"Just the fact that you don't want to say them is why you should. Why do we have to play games with each other? I always say that I'm sorry, but both of us know that I'm not always the one who should say it. And sometimes I'm not sorry at all. It's only a signal to get you started on making up with me. Isn't it silly?"

There are circumstances in a husband-and-wife relationship that can cause the same person to always be the one to patch things up or to get them back on track. The other party gets used to it, so he never has to face into himself and admit to his spouse that he has been wrong. It is not a good situation. Sometimes the excuse is, "Well, it's better than just staying mad," or, "Maybe it isn't fair that I have to give in all the time, but at least we're at

"We" are more important than anything.

139

peace." That's true. But there's another choice. A couple can sit down and honestly talk to each other about the one-sided situation and why it is not good.

If I am always trying to make up, then the entire relationship is one of "making up." I have not sought forgiveness, and the relationship has not grown any deeper. I have responded to your unwillingness to give in. I figure I might as well give in and coddle you back to good humor. We'll get it over with and start fresh. That's just trying to smooth out the problem. It does little for us.

It's quite an unworkable situation if one person is always the sinner and the other person always the saint. Both of us are sinners; both of us have occasion to seek forgiveness.

How does your healing each other through forgiveness affect your coupleness?

Your answer:

Karl was on Miriam's blacklist. She was furious with him for letting their son Tim have the car after she had said no. She knew Karl would be wanting to talk to her in a few minutes and she didn't want to talk to him. She was mad and enjoying her mad. The more she thought about what Karl had *done* the more livid she became. And she knew that if she started thinking about Karl as a *person* she'd cool off. That would be horrible. But why? Being boiling mad wasn't all that enjoyable.

She really wanted to stay mad but what good would that do her? So she started to think about Karl. He had such a tender heart and he was so generous. He'd give you the shirt off his back. That's why he had given the car to Tim. Karl was very understanding of Tim and of her. He never blamed her for her moods and quick temper. She looked at him, so hurt since she yelled at him. She couldn't resist going over, sitting beside him and saying,

"You're out of the doghouse. Oh, honey, how I love you!"

Forgiveness brings us close together and cements our relationship. It makes us aware of each other's goodness. The person who has been forgiven is overwhelmed and awed by the mercifulness and the generosity of his beloved. The person who is extending forgiveness is thunderstruck by his partner's humility and love. Once we have forgiven each other, life will never again be the same between us.

Each time of forgiveness is a moment of maturing in a marriage. It is a coming of age and an advancement. It makes us both realize the potential we have in each other.

Forgiveness is a testimony to our experience of unity. Rather than just avoiding hurts in our relationship or doing the right thing by each other or living up to our responsibilities, we are reaching out for an integration of our two selves. We are intermingling our souls. Nothing has greater significance for a husband-and-wife relationship than our experience of forgiving and being forgiven by each other.

What part does touching play in forgiveness?   *Your answer:*

Forgiveness seldom takes place without touching. When we think of the story of the Prodigal Son we can't picture the moment of reconciliation without seeing the father with his arms around his boy.

I express my forgiveness to you with my whole being. When I seek forgiveness I need the protection and strength that your arm around me provides.

Forgiveness is not something done simply with words. It's a personal expression, both in the seeking and in the granting. Our whole personhood is involved in that moment. The words in themselves are so magnificent, so overwhelming, that they are almost incredible without the reality of touch. When you ask me to forgive you, your touch tells me you care. When I ask you to forgive me and you graciously grant me the totality of forgiveness, it becomes most credible when I feel it through your hand on my shoulder, your face against mine. Truly, touching gives substance to forgiveness.

Do you talk about what forgiveness has meant to you?

Your answer:

Forgiveness is a wonderful experience and we appreciate it, but we don't enjoy the great moments of forgiveness as we could. We can relive those experiences and keep gaining from them! They need not grow dim in our memory. We can fondle them in our minds, go over them in our hearts and talk about them together. Without sharing our feelings concerning the seeking and granting of forgiveness we won't have anywhere near the awareness of how much they have meant.

One Sunday morning Joel and Karen were having a cup of coffee and just talking back and forth. Joel asked Karen what she most remembered about them as a couple. "That's too big to answer off the top of my head," she answered. "Let me have a little time to think it over and I'll jot some things down."

About a half hour later Karen was back with several filled pages. She passed them to Joel.

"I could write a book about our love but the time that still gets to me is how gentle and forgiving you were with me over sex. Remember how horrible I was? Everything about sex was for *me;* I had to be pleased. I made you so guilty about failing me. I reacted against sex being a man's thing. Life must have been hell for you.

"You stuck with me. I was really impossible. When it suited me I was 'Miss Old-fashioned Feminity' and on other occasions I was a hard-core libber. I was so selfish I never considered you at all. I finally realized what I was doing and got enough courage to ask you to forgive me. I can still remember the look of tenderness in your eyes and the way you kissed me gently and said, 'Don't blame yourself. Let's forget the past. Just know how much you are loved.'

"So often, Joel, I think of that moment. How much confidence it gives me in your love, how reassured I am whenever I fail you, knowing that you won't hold it against me. Your only thought was of how I was feeling. You weren't thinking of yourself at all, just of me. I can never forget how you healed me. Without your over-whelming love I would have found it impossible to forgive myself."

Joel was so moved he held onto her hand and pressed it against his cheek. "I never knew you remembered that time or that it meant anything to you. Thanks for telling me."

One of the greatest gifts we can bestow on our husbands and wives is to give them a true sense of how much they mean to us, how much they have contributed to our lives, how our whole world is different because of our relationship with them. Talking over our forgiveness is a tremendous way to make them experience how precious they are in our consciousness.

Too often we spend our time together talking about inconsequential things, and yet the real power of our relationship is right on the tips of our tongues if we'll only release it. Talking over the marvelous experiences of forgiveness can wonderfully deepen a couple's relationship.

What is the most difficult consequence of forgiving your beloved?

Your answer:

Probably the most difficult facet of forgiveness is forgetting. If I am fully forgiving you, I'm telling you, "From this moment on, I will remember, not my hurt, but your goodness in seeking my forgiveness." When we only *excuse* one another we maintain the right to remember what was done to us and what effect it had on us. When we *forgive* we give up that right. That's the most magnificent thing about forgiveness.

Of course it is natural for us to be tempted into saying, "Well, I can't control my memory. I can't help it if I remember what you did to me or how badly it pains me." But the fact is we *do* have control over our memory. We can train ourselves to remember certain things. Our memory is selective. We don't remember everything. We remember what we're interested in and what most affects us. So if we remember the pain, we're saying that the pain affected us more than the humility and beauty of the person who seeks our forgiveness.

We can train our memory so that whenever we think of the unfortunate event that occurred, the consequence that most comes to our mind is not the pain but the tremendous closeness and beauty of the other person in forgiveness. If we don't, we have to seek forgiveness for not having accomplished forgiveness in the first place! And we have to work on our memory.

I can say to myself that the pain was so searing when you said that to me, or when you ignored me for such a long period of time, that I can't forget it. If I do I have decided to keep it lodged in my mind. If I remember the hurt rather than the reality of your asking forgiveness, then there's something wrong in me. The only way it can be healed is by *my* seeking forgiveness of you for considering an event or a situation to be more important than you. I can purposely recall the overwhelming presence of you at that moment when you said to me, "I really need you—not to excuse me, not just to straighten things out between us—but to forgive me."

With forgiveness there is healing and light hearts! Life is rich and joyous!